FAMILY WALKS
IN SOUTH
YORKSHIRE

GW00471480

Norman Taylor

Distributed by NMD, Sheffield S13 9NP
Phone: 0800 834920

FAMILY WALKS
IN SOUTH YORKSHIRE

THE COUNTRY CODE

Guard against all risk of fire
Fasten all gates
Keep dogs under proper control
Keep to paths across farm land
Avoid damaging fences, hedges and walls
Leave no litter
Safeguard water supplies
Protect wildlife, wild plants and trees
Go carefully along country roads
Respect the life of the countryside

Published 2005

© Norman Taylor 2005

No part of this book may be reproduced in any form or by any means without the permission of the owner of the Copyright.

ISBN 0 907758 25 8

Stepping Stones, Low Bradfield

Acknowledgements

I am greatly indebted to Barry Pope for the time and effort he has devoted to revising and improving the maps used in this edition. Without Barry's and his wife Maureen's input, this revision of walks, in an area that is sadly neglected by walking guides, might have been shelved.

I am deeply grateful to John and Freda Hill for checking out the walks for this revised edition. Features change as time passes, and there is always room for improvement. Their constructive criticism and suggestions for amendment were welcome and are incorporated in this edition of the guide.

I must also thank my son Sam and Tim Brown for making a special effort in providing photographs for this edition of the guide.

Mill Pond, Loxley Valley

CONTENTS

Map of the area showing locations of walks 4

Introduction 5

Map Symbols 8

The Walks

1. Cannon Hall, Deffer Wood and Cawthorne *(4.75 miles)* 9
2. Kine Moor and Silkstone Fall *(5 miles)* 13
3. Royd Moor and Hartcliff Hill *(6 miles)* 17
4. Worsborough Mill Country Park *(1.5, 2.25, 2.5, or 4.5 miles)* 21
5. Langsett Reservoir and Midhope Moor *(3.5 or 5 miles)* 25
6. Green Moor and Upper Don Valley *(2.25, 3 or 4.5 miles)* 29
7. Mill Moor, Hermit Hill and Wortley Park *(5.5 miles)* 33
8. Bolsterstone and Whitwell Moor *(4 or 5 miles)* 37
9. Spout House Hill and Hollin Edge Height *(4, 4.75 or 6 miles)* 41
10. Bradfield Dale and Dale Dike Reservoir *(4.5 miles)* 45
11. Loxley Valley *(1.25, 2.75 or 4.5 miles)* 49
12. Rivelin Valley *(2.5 or 4 miles)* 53
13. Burbage Valley *(2.5 or 4.5 miles)* 57
14. Dearne Valley and Barnburgh *(5.5 miles)* 61
15. Roche Abbey and Laughton-en-le-Morthen *(1.5 or 4.5 miles)* 65
16. Chesterfield Canal: Shireoaks to Thorpe Salvin *(3.5 or 4.5 miles)* 69

Appendices

— Routes in order of difficulty 73

— Country Parks 74

— Nature Reserves 74

— Museums and Places of Historical Interest 75

3

MAP OF THE AREA
Numbers 1 to 16 indicate the Location of the Walks

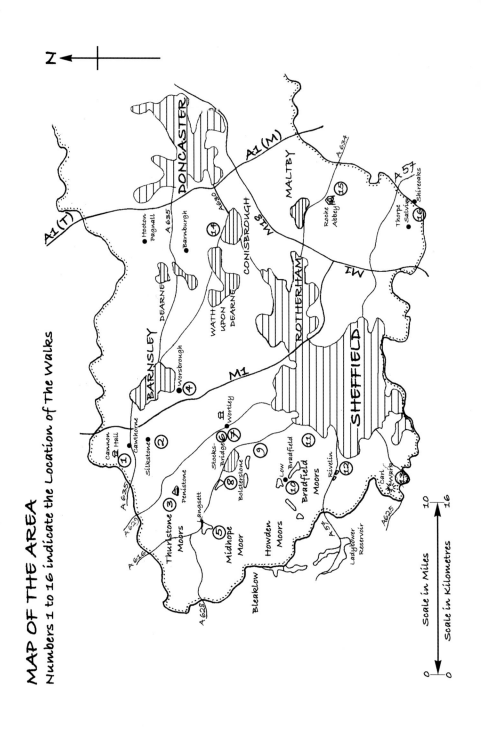

Scale in Miles

Scale in Kilometres

Introduction

The walks in this guide follow the same formula as those in my Peak District guides. They are all in attractive countryside. Most important of all, they were worked out to suit the interests and stamina of children, although they are not exclusive to families, and many other walkers may find this book suited to their taste. The more strenuous parts of a walk are nearly always within the first half, with easier, often downhill walking to complete the journey. Road-walking is kept to a minimum, and where it is unavoidable only short sections are involved. All the walks have several focal points which both break up the journey and are attractive to children, such as woods, streams, ponds and weirs, rocks to scramble on, trees to climb, historical relics to explore, interesting wildlife and good picnic spots. In addition, where possible the walks happen on a wayside inn or tea-shop roughly midway along.

As for the area covered by this guide, it may come as a surprise to some that South Yorkshire has, as well as its conurbations and industry , a lot of beautiful countryside. The west of the county is characterised by high moorland, gritstone crags, reservoirs and pine forests much of which lie within the Peak District National Park. Going eastwards, the landscape changes to one of rolling countryside with wooded hillsides and valleys, and rivers and streams alongside which are many relics of past water-powered industries. Beyond the urban and industrial development in the central area, the terrain is more gently undulating. This, in combination with its rich and fertile soils has meant that the area has been prime agricultural land for centuries, and within it there are many ancient settlements and interesting antiquities to explore.

A quick glance at the map opposite will reveal that the majority of the walks are in the west of the county. As well as being a reflection of my own preference for variety in landscape when out walking, an important requirement was that the walks have sufficient interest en route for children. I hope my selection meets this requirement. More than this, I hope that others get as much pleasure exploring South Yorkshire on foot as I did

Choosing a walk

Unless the children taking part are seasoned walkers, it is best not to be too ambitious at first; walking along uneven footpaths or scaling a hillside is hard going if you are not used to it. In the case of very young children, start with the very short walks, and even then be prepared to turn back. The aim is to introduce them to the joys of the countryside and not to put them off walking forever! When a full walk is planned, it is a good idea to make contingency plans, so that if the party gets halfway along a route and the youngsters are on the point of rebellion, rescue can be arranged by meeting motorised friends at the pub en route or by one of the adults hurrying back to collect the transport.

To help in choosing a walk, I have listed the walks in order of difficulty at the back of the book.

Allowing sufficient time

Each walk is intended as the best part of a day's outing, allowing time for play, exploration and rest stops. It is better to overestimate rather than underestimate the time it may take, and then have to 'route march' the latter part of the journey. As a rough guide, allow apace of around a mile per hour for the younger child, graduating to two miles per hour for the experienced eleven year old. Where hill-climbing is involved, add on extra time dependent on the size and fitness of the children in the party.

What to wear

British weather being what it is, it is best to go prepared for the worst, and even on a dry day there is always the chance that a youngster will end up soaked if the walk follows a stream. For the grown-ups, a good pair of lightweight walking boots are recommended if you want to keep your feet dry. At the same time, they provide ankle support along rough terrain and a better grip on slippery footpaths. Walking boots are also recommended for children and are now widely available. Waterproof outer clothes are essential for every member of the party. The cagoule is especially useful since it is also windproof, light and easy to pack in a rucksack. The same goes for over-trousers. A spare sweater for the youngsters is advisable, and a complete change of clothing is a must for the more accident prone little ones.

Footpaths and rights of way

All the walks in this guide use public rights of way or paths that have been made available for use by the general public. Although in most cases footpaths are well-defined, there are a few exceptions where, because of infrequent use, the way ahead is not very obvious. However, the routes are described in sufficient detail for this not to pose insurmountable problems in route finding. From time to time, farmers have been known to block off a stile on a right of way. In the unlikely event of this happening, use your initiative, avoiding damage to fences and walls, and report the matter to myself or the Rambler's Association. Where a right of way has been ploughed, you should continue in the direction of the right of way even if this means treading on

6

crops. There are two reasons for this. Firstly, the farmer is required by law to make good the surface of a right of way subsequent to ploughing and sowing. Secondly, by making a detour around a crop, you are venturing off the right of way on to private land.

The maps

The maps in this guide, in combination with the route descriptions, are sufficiently detailed to be used without reference to other maps of the area. Nevertheless, many walkers will wish to take the standard Ordnance Survey sheets with them, and appropriate grid references are given for each route

Refreshments

All the walks have pubs or teashops en route. If you intend buying pub food, it is as well to check before setting out the time bar meals are served. Teashop opening times vary according to the time of year and expected volume of custom but most can be relied on to be open until late afternoon in the summer season.

Transport to the area

Although I have assumed that most people will travel to the area by car, South Yorkshire's comprehensive bus service should enable one to get to the start points of most of the walks in this guide.

GOLDENEYE
black and white with green head - 46cm

Symbols used on the route maps

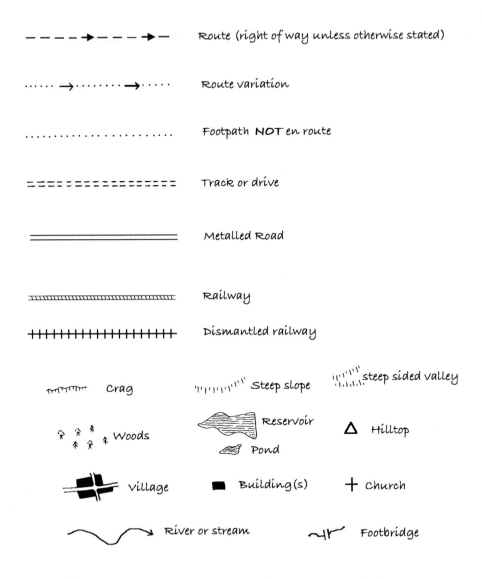

– – – – ➤ – – – ➤ –   Route (right of way unless otherwise stated)

······ → ········· → ·····   Route variation

·   Footpath **NOT** en route

= = = = = = = = = = = = = = = = =   Track or drive

——————————————   Metalled Road

ⲧⲧⲧⲧⲧⲧⲧⲧⲧⲧⲧⲧⲧⲧⲧⲧⲧⲧⲧⲧⲧⲧⲧⲧⲧⲧⲧ   Railway

+++++++++++++++++++++++   Dismantled railway

ⲧⲧⲧⲧⲧⲧ Crag   ᵗⁱᵗᵢ Steep slope   ᵗⁱᵗⁱ steep sided valley

🌲🌲🌲🌲 Woods   Reservoir   △ Hilltop
                      Pond

Village   ▪ Building(s)   + Church

River or stream   ⤳⊦ Footbridge

④ etc. Number corresponds with route description

Cannon Hall, Deffer Wood and Cawthorne

Outline   Cannon Hall - Jowett House - Deffer Wood - Hoyland Hill
- Cawthorne - Cannon Hall

Summary   An excellent walk in the rolling countryside northwest of
Barnsley, taking in woodland, open pastures, parkland and including a
visit to the picturesque and historically interesting village of Cawthorne. A
mixture of forest tracks, field footpaths and country lanes are used as far as
Cawthorne, and the last half mile is a pleasant stroll through Cannon Hall
Country Park. All the hard work is concentrated in the first mile and a half,
which leads to the top of a ridge above Deffer Wood. From this point, there
is a fine view of the surrounding country.

Attractions A little way up from the car park is Cannon Hall Museum. The
hall was the family home of the Spencers, entrepreneurs in the manufacture
of iron during the 17th and 18th centuries. The building dates from the late
1600's although it was remodelled by John Carr of York between 1765 and
1784. The lovely parkland was landscaped by Richard Woods and Thomas
Peach in the 1760's.

   Another interesting building in the vicinity is Jowett House Mill,
situated on the opposite side of the road just across the bridge. Now a
private residence, it was a water-driven corn mill from the mid 17th to the
mid 19th centuries, when it was converted to a sawmill for the estate and
continued to be used as such until the 1950's.

   About half a mile from the start of the walk, Deffer Wood is entered
by a narrow footpath that winds it way through a dense stretch of young
woodland. Here, sycamore, ash, oak, scots pine and birch are in competition
with a shrub layer of hawthorn, bracken, rhododendron and wild rosehip.
Once through this rather wonderful wilderness, a wide forest track leads
uphill through tall pines, where there are ample opportunities for a wayside
picnic or a bit of en route hide-and-seek.

   After climbing out of the woodland a lane is followed along the broad
crest of a ridge, from which the views are particularly good. Dominating
the skyline to the northwest is the giant T. V. mast on Emley Moor. On
leaving the ridge, a descent is made through more woodland and across
meadows, where lapwing and partridge may be seen. An old coach road
is then followed up into Cawthorne, a most attractive village with a long
history.

   Its origins date back to Anglo-Saxon times at least, since Cawthorne waa
already an established settlement when it was entered in Domesday Book.

continued on page 12

9

Route 1

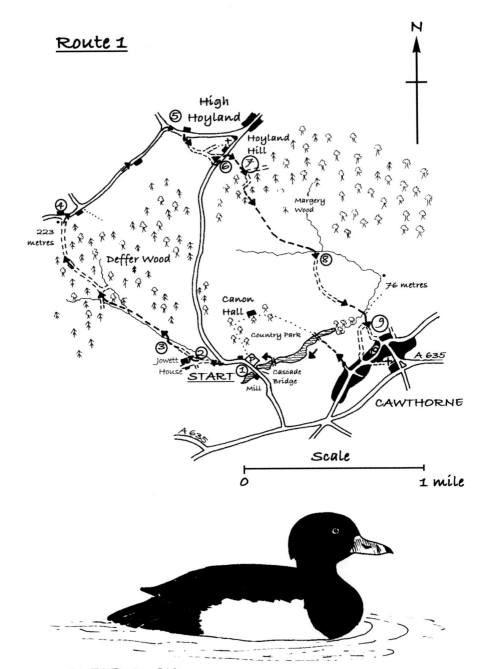

N

High
Hoyland ⑤

Hoyland
Hill

⑥ ⑦

Margery
Wood

④

223
metres

Deffer Wood

⑧

76 metres

Canon
Hall

⑨

Country Park

③ ②

Jowett
House

START ①

Mill

Cascade
Bridge

A 635

CAWTHORNE

A 635

Scale

0   1 mile

TUFTED DUCK
black and white - 43cm

10

Route 1

Cannon Hall, Deffer Wood and Cawthorne 4 ¾miles

START *At Cannon Hall Country Park. Leave the A635, Barnsley to Denby Dale road, west of Cawthorne and go north to Cascade Bridge and the car park. (G.R. 273079)*

ROUTE

1. *From the car park, walk back to the road and turn right. Follow the road round a left-hand bend and as far as a sharp right-hand bend. Leave the road here, and take the lane signposted to Jowett House Farm.*

2. *On reaching the farm, fork right along a track and continue through a gate into a field. Bear right, keeping a fence on the right, and reach a gate with a stile.*

3. *Cross the stile and turn left, keeping close to a hedge and stream on the left. On reaching another stile, cross this and follow the meandering footpath through woodland to meet up with forest tracks. Ignoring other possibilities, continue straight on along a wide forest track, which climbs steadily through the wood and eventually reaches a country lane.*

4. *Turn right and follow the lane to a fork. continue to a T-junction (about 2/3mile).*

5. *Take the right fork and Turn right here and follow the lane for about 200 metres to a Public Footpath sign on the right, opposite a farm. Go right, then immediately left through a gateway to follow a disused track that has degenerated to a footpath. Continue along this, forking right at signs, to the road at Hoyland Hill.*

6. *Turn left and go to a stile on the right signposted to Cawthorne. Cross the stile and go straight down a field to another stile at the entrance to Margery Wood, where there are two footpath signs.*

7. *Continue straight ahead downhill. In 100 metres follow the forest track bending to the right. Stay on this track, ignoring other possibilities to left and right, and follow it after it has degenerated to a footpath, where it bears left into the woods. This footpath leads to a gate and stile at the edge of the wood (yellow arrow). Continue across a field to another way-marked stile, then bear half-left down a large field to a third way-marked stile in the fence on the left. Cross this and bear half-right to the far corner of the field ahead to reach a gate with a stile on the right of it.*

8. *Continue uphill along a farm track, cross a stone stepping-stile on the left of a gate and, with a fence on your left, carry on to a way-marked stile. Cross it and continue to a T -junction of paths.*

9. *Turn right and follow the path up into Cawthorne.*

Although the church is Norman, built in the early part of the 13th century, it replaced a Saxon church that probably stood on the same spot. Its tower was added in the late 15th or early 16th century. The Spencer Arms, whilst having more immediate appeal, is also an interesting building. It was originally a farm owned by the Spencer family and their coat-of-arms is boldly displayed on the front of the building. During the 18th century the farm was converted to a coaching inn. The stables were underneath the present restaurant. Cawthorne has its own museum, which is worth a visit. A little way on from the museum, on the right, is an old stone cottage with a large, flat metal circle in the pavement in front of it. This was a smithy from the early 1800's until 1956. The metal circle was used to fit hot metal bands on to the outer rims of cartwheels.

Leaving Cawthorne, Cannon Hall Country Park is entered. This is a delightful place where children can roam freely and explore the life of the ponds. These support a variety of water birds including pochard, tufted duck, goldeneye, mute swan, barnacle, greylag and Canada geese, all of which will finish off unwanted morsels of the packed lunch

Refreshments   Spencer Arms at Cawthorne.

---

10. *Turn right in the village. (The Spencer Arms is left then first right. To regain the route, go through the churchyard opposite the pub and continue down a tree-lined avenue). Pass Cawthorne Club and continue to "The Park", a road on the right. Follow this to its end, then continue along a footpath leading into Cannon Hall Country Park. Go left by the string of ponds to reach the car park.*

Marsh Marigold
(yellow)   March - August

Kine Moor and Silkstone Fall

Outline   Silkstone Common ~ Lindley Wood ~ Silkstone ~ Fall Head ~ Silkstone Fall ~ Champany Hill ~ Silkstone Common

Summary   A fine ramble amidst the peaceful, attractive countryside of the ancient parish of Silkstone. The walk passes through a mixture of farmland and woodland, some of which is a relic of a large forest that once covered this area. About halfway round the old pit village of Silkstone is visited. From the highest point on the walk, on Champany Hill, there are extensive views of the surrounding countryside. A combination of footpaths and tracks are used throughout.

Attractions   Situated between the urban development of Barnsley to the east and the high moorland to the west, the area around Silkstone is characterised by gently rolling hills and valleys clothed in fields and woodland. Much of this is natural and a relic of the ancient forest that once covered these foothills of the central Pennines.   Soon after leaving Silkstone Common, footpaths and tracks lead to Lindley Wood, a small stretch of secluded woodland with a stream running through it. Oak, pine and sycamore reach high in competition for light and, since their foliage is also high, sufficient sunlight filters through to the ground to create an ideal habitat for ferns, blackberries, bluebells and many other woodland wild flowers. A little further on, wall bedstraw and devilsbit scabious take advantage of the more open locations on the edges of fields where the plough cannot reach them .

To the east of Silkstone, an approach road to Bull Haw Hall Farm is used. One of the earliest references to coal-mining in South Yorkshire is contained in inquests held during the reign of Edward I. One of these inquests, in 1293, concerned a man who met his death whilst digging coal near his home at Bull Haw. In 1838, a terrible tragedy occurred in mining the same rich coal seam, when 26 children aged from 7 to 17 years were drowned after Silkstone coalmine flooded. There is a monument to the children in the churchyard at Silkstone.

As for the church itself, this dates from around the beginning of the 13th century. Its western tower, built in 1495, replaced an older central tower. A little way down from the church, adjacent to the Ring 0' Bells public house, are Silkstone stocks, which have been reconstructed around the original stone supports.

continued on page 6

Route 2

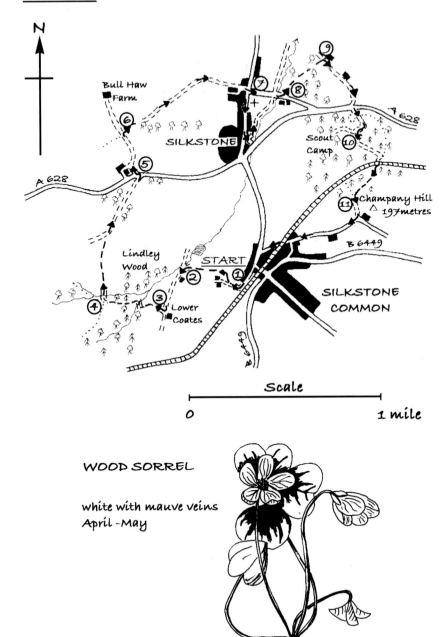

N

Bull Haw
Farm

⑥

⑦

⑧

⑨

SILKSTONE

Scout
Camp

⑩

A 628

A 628

⑤

⑪ Champany Hill
△ 197 metres

B 6449

Lindley
Wood

START

②

①

SILKSTONE
COMMON

③ Lower
Coates

④

B 6449

Scale

0   1 mile

WOOD SORREL

white with mauve veins
April - May

Route 2

Kine Moor and Silkstone Fall   5 miles

START   *At Silkstone Common, about 4 miles west of Barnsley. Park at the station car park or nearby. To get to the car park, take the road signposted to Silkstone, turning left immediately after passing under the railway bridge. The street is a cul-de-sac. (G.R. 290043)*

ROUTE

1. *Continue on from the car park towards the housing estate, then turn right along a track (Public Footpath sign). Walk down the track as far as a gateway on the right of which is a way-marked stile. Cross this and a second stile, then keep close to the hedge on the right. Leave the hedge where it turns right and continue straight down the field to the start of a farm-track at a gate with a stile on the left.*

2. *Bear left with the track to a junction with another track. Bear left again and continue uphill, passing a private dwelling on the left. Go as far as a stile on the fight immediately before a farm (Lower Coates) .*

3. *Turn right to cross the stile and, keeping a hedge on the right, continue to a stile on the edge of Lindley Wood. Cross this and carry on down to and across a footbridge, then bear left uphill through the wood. The footpath crosses a grassy track and then follows a wall on the left. Keep on this footpath as far as a stone stile in the wall on the left.*

4. *Turn right at this point and follow a less well-defined footpath through a narrow strip of the wood. Continue over a footbridge and˙ through a handgate to a field. Keeping a hedge on the right, walk along the field edge, crossing a section of open field where part of the hedge has been removed. Continue over a stile and, still with a hedge on the right, keep straight on to a junction with a farm track. Follow this, still going in the same direction, to reach a road (A628).*

5. *Turn left, then right at the lane signposted Bull Haw Hall Farm. Follow the lane round aright-hand bend then a left-hand bend. About 300 metres past the left-hand bend a way-marked stile on the left is reached. Opposite this, but not so obvious, is a stone stile.*

6. *Turn right here and cross the stone stile. Continue straight on down to a stile and a track at the left-hand corner of a wood. After crossing the stile, turn right and follow the track into Silkstone. (For the Red Lion and Ring-o-Bells, turn right at the main road. To rejoin the route, turn left off the road by the stocks adjacent to the Ring-o- Bells, then turn left again to follow a track to the main road at Pot House Bridge. Turn*

On leaving Silkstone, the walk back is mainly through woodland, some of which is natural and some man-made. The walking along this section is particularly pleasant, and there is plenty of interest for the keen naturalist. Just as exciting for the youngsters, the footpath crosses a railway line halfway up Silkstone Fall. This is a well-used branch line, however, and children should be closely supervised in crossing it.

Once out of the woods, the route nears the summit of Champany Hill before heading off downhill back to Silkstone Common. The views along this last section are well worth the climb up through the woods.

Refreshments   Red Lion, Silkstone. Beer garden.

---

right and continue up the road to a Public Footpath sign on the left. Continue as for 8.)

7. *On reaching the main road in Silkstone, turn right, then left to follow the Dodworth road down past the church. After passing Pot House Mill Farm on the right, a Public Footpath sign on the left is soon reached.*

8. *Turn left here, then bear right up a disused grassy track through a wood. Where the track bends sharply to the right, leave it and continue ascending in more or less the same direction along a footpath. This ends at the far corner of the wood at a track.*

9. *Turn right and follow the track past two groups of farm buildings to reach the Silkstone to Dodworth road. Cross the road and continue along the woodland track opposite (signposted Silverwood Scout Camp) . Ignoring a right fork to a turning circle, follow the track to the second right-hand bend.*

10. *Leave the Scout Camp access track at this point. Instead, go straight ahead along a narrower track that winds uphill to a foot-crossing over a railway line. Once across this, turn right and follow a footpath uphill through a plantation to a T-junction of footpaths.*

11. *Turn left and continue to lane-. Turn right at the lane and follow it down to its end at the railway track in Silkstone Common. Turn left along a public footpath, go under the railway and then left to finish.*

Royd Moor and Hartcliff Hill

Outline   Thurlstone ~ Royd Moor Reservoir ~ Royd Moor Hill ~ Bullhouse Mill ~ Ecklands ~ Hartcliff Hill ~ Thurlstone

Summary   A fairly strenuous though rewarding walk with variety and particularly fine views in the hilly Pennine countryside west of Peniston . Starting in the village of Thurlstone, a combination of tracks and footpaths lead to the secluded reservoir on Royd Moor and then to the top of a broad ridge. From here, field footpaths, parts of which are little used, are followed back down into the valley to cross the River Don. The next mile and a half involves a fairly stiff climb, albeit in stages, to the summit of Hartcliff Hill. At 1100 feet above sea level, it is probably the best viewpoint in the area. Tracks and footpaths lead to this high point, after which a descent to Thurlstone is made along a bridleway.

Attractions Although Thurlstone grew as a result of the development of the textile industries alongside the River Don, it is a village with ancient origins, named after Thurl, a Danish chieftain. The suffix 'ton', sometimes spelt with an 'e', is Old English for a farmstead but was later applied to hamlets and, eventually, villages. The narrow field strips to the north of Thurlstone are evidence of strip farming in medieval times, the walls being added in the late 17th century.

A mile out of Thurlstone, a footpath is followed past Royd Moor Reservoir which, with its borders of sedges, reeds and wild flowers, more closely resembles a natural lake than a man-made reservoir. Its seclusion makes it an ideal habitat for water birds. As well as grebe, tufted duck, coot and mallard, less common species, some migrants amongst these, are attracted to this quiet location.

Leaving the waterside, a short trek uphill through meadow land leads to the summit of Royd Moor Hill at 1083 feet, and from here there is a fine view across the U upper Don Valley to Hartcliff Hill.

After a steep descent through grazing land, the Don is crossed at Bullhouse Mill. A little way up a disused track is Bullhouse Farm, originally a hall built by the Riches in 1655 and enlarged in 1688. Nearby, and in the same grounds, is a chapel erected by the family in 1692.

On leaving this attractive little setting, a steep ascent leads to the tiny hamlet of Ecklands, where goats are more common than sheep. The climb continues to the bridle path below the summit of Hartcliff Hill. The ascent from the bridlepath is steep and strenuous but the effort is

continued on page 20

17

Route 3

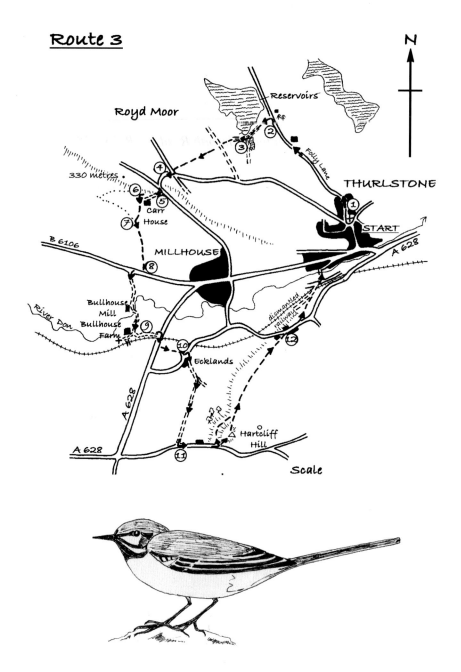

N

Royd Moor

Reservoirs

330 metres

THURLSTONE

Folly Lane

START

B 6106

Carr House

MILLHOUSE

A 628

Bullhouse Mill

River Don

Bullhouse Farm

dismantled railway

A 628

Ecklands

A 628

Hartcliff Hill

Scale

Grey Wagtail   Blue-grey above with yellow-green rump and yellow beneath.

Route 3

Royd Moor and Hartcliff Hill   6 miles

START   *In Thurlstone, a mile west of Penistone. Turn north off the A628 by the Post Office on the main road through Thurlstone. The street is Towngate. Park considerately in the village, then locate the Baptist Chapel on Ingbirchworth Road. (G.R. 233038)*

ROUTE

1. *Walk up Ingbirchworth Road and on to Folly Lane. Continue along Folly Lane for about 2/3 mile to a stile on the left before a Yorkshire Water Authority sign*

2. *Cross the stile and another a little further on, then continue around the edge of the reservoir.*

3. *Turn right and go over a footbridge. (The steps and footpath to the right lead to the reservoir edge.) Continue over two way-marked stiles, then go up the field ahead, bearing half right to a stile . Cross this, then keep straight on until you join a road.*

4. *Turn left at the road, then sharp right at the junction ahead, and walk downhill to a T -junction.*

5. *Turn left, then take the first track on the right (Public Footpath sign), which descends to farm buildings (Carr House).*

6. *Fork right just above the farm along a track used only by livestock, and which is bordered by a wall on the left. Follow the wall for about 100 metres to an old stile on the left. Go through it then down over rough ground (no footpath) to an old gatepost to the right of the farmhouse . Continue in the same direction, passing between the farmhouse and an outbuilding, then bear left down a field to a wooden footbridge and a stile. Go across a narrow field (no footpath) to reach a stone stile.*

7. *After crossing the stile, turn left, follow the wall for a short distance, then bear right across a large field to reach the main road.*

8. *Turn right at the road and follow it for a short distance to a lane on the left (Public Bridleway). Follow the lane past a house and Bullhouse Mill, then continue across a bridge over the River Don. Follow the disused track up to the right to reach the lane that leads to Bullhouse Farm on the right.*

9. *Turn left and walk along the lane to a main road (A628) . Turn right at the road and, in a short distance, cross over to an iron gate (Public Footpath sign)*

rewarded by an exceptional view of the surrounding countryside and, in particular, the higher Pennine moorland to the west. The summit is also an ideal spot to picnic, since it is wild and overgrown and provides plenty of scope for play and exploration. The bridlepath down to Thurlstone follows the course of a medieval saltway. Salt, a particularly valuable commodity in the days before refrigeration, was transported by packhorse from the salt 'wiches' in Cheshire across the Pennines to the medieval market towns in the east.

Refreshments Crystal Palace at Thurlstone. Beer garden.

Go through the gate, then, at right angles to the road, cross a field, a stile and stone footbridge and climb steeply 'alongside a wall on the right. Go over a stile at the top of the incline, pass right of a house via the garden. Turn right to reach the minor road that passes through Ecklands.

10. *Turn left at the road, then right at a track that passes behind houses. Continue uphill along the track, going right where it forks. Follow it to a minor road.*

11. *Turn left at the road and follow this for ¼ mile to a Public Bridleway sign on the left. Either follow the bridleway around the summit of Hartcliff Hill or fork right off it and climb steeply to its summit. From the top, bear left along a narrow footpath, continue through a gap in the wall on the left, and descend to join the bridleway. Follow the bridleway down to a road at Bank House Farm.*

12. *Turn right and walk up the road to a Public Footpath on the left (signposted). Follow the path down to a track. Turn right and follow this across a disused railway to a road. Turn right, then go left at a footpath on the left. Follow this over a footbridge over the Don. Continue past a coal merchant's and to the main road in Thurlstone. Turn right, then left at the Post Office to finish.*

(Shorter Variations 2½,2¼ and 1½miles)

Worsbrough Mill Country Park

Outline   Worsbrough Mill - Broom Royd Wood - Rockley Abbey Farm - Worsbrough - Worsbrough Mill

Summary   Without the intrusion of a motorway and its associated noise pollution this would be a first rate walk. As it stands, it nevertheless a worthy inclusion to this guide, with plenty of historical interest, variety and an excursion through countryside that remains largely unaffected by the busy thoroughfare that cuts through A combination of footpaths and tracks are used, all of which are well-defined. Several features of historical interest are passed en route.

Attractions   The walk starts by Worsbrough Reservoir and Worsbrough Mill Museum, which is well worth a visit. A corn mill on this site is mentioned in the Domesday Book of 1086, although the present watermill was built in 1625. In the mid 19th century, with the development of the coal and iron industry in the area, the steam-powered mill was added to meet the increased demand for flour and meal. With the introduction of new roller mills and mass-produced white flour towards the end of the 19th century , the mill's trade declined and the steam engine was scrapped, although the watermill continued grinding corn for animal feed until the 1960's. The mill has since been fully restored as an industrial museum and operates most days.

    The Country Park passed through in the early stages of the walk includes the reservoir, wetland, deciduous woodland and grassland. The reservoir's enlargement in 1806 produced an area of shallow water at the western end, where willow carr and reed beds have established themselves. On this western edge an observation hide has been constructed to view the rich birdlife hereabouts, which includes pochard, great crested grebe, heron and many more species.

    After crossing over the M1, the noise of the traffic soon grows dim and is left behind for a while as the walk weaves its way through the picturesque rolling countryside to the west of the motorway. Here, there is a more or less even distribution of farmland and woodland which, together, support a rich variety of flora and fauna.

    Near Rockley Farm, peering out above the trees that are threatening to obscure it from view altogether, is Rockley Engine House. Built in 1813, this tower-like building drained local ironstone workings. Nearby. and totally concealed by the trees around it, is Rockley blast furnace.

continued on page 24

Route 4

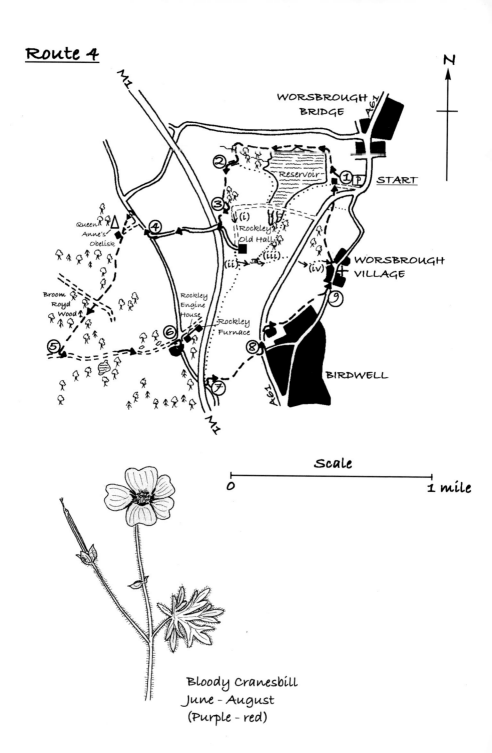

Bloody Cranesbill
June - August
(Purple - red)

Route 4

Worsbrough Mill Country Park 4½ miles

(Shorter Variations 2½,2¼ and 1½miles)

START   *Park at the official car park for Worsbrough Mill Country Park, half way between Barnsley and Birdwell on the A61. (G.R. 352033)*

ROUTE

1. *From the car park walk to the Mill, then cross to the other side of the reservoir via the footpath along the top of the dam or the one below it. Turn left and continue alongside the reservoir, bearing left where there are other possibilities. After crossing a footbridge on the west of the reservoir, walk on for about 100metres only to where there is a footbridge on the right of the main footpath.*

2. *Turn right here, cross the footbridge and a stile, and follow a field footpath as far as a bend in a track.*

3. *Turn right and, keeping a hedge on your right, walk around the field boundary to reach a bridge over the motorway. Cross it and follow a lane to a T-junction.*

4. *Turn right and continue on the road, passing a private drive on the left, to a stile on the left signposted to Green Springs. Cross the stile and bear left across a field to a stile and the aforementioned drive. Cross them both and go through the kissing gate opposite. Continue to a stile, after which the footpath bears right across a field to the edge of a wood. Follow the path alongside the wood. When a track is reached, go straight across to a stile and continue through a stretch of woodland (Broom Royd Wood). Stay on this footpath, ignoring a stile on the right, to reach a track.*

5. *Turn left at the track and follow it to a road, passing a caravan site en route. (Rockley Engine House and Rockley Furnace are accessible via a footpath on the opposite side of the road.)*

6. *Turn right and walk along the road and under the motorway to a track on the left signposted to Rockley Old Hall.*

7. *Follow this track for a few metres to a wooden stile on the right. Cross this and continue uphill with a hedge on the left. Before reaching the top of the field, pass through an open gateway on the left and continue, now with a hedge on the right, to a main road (A61).*

8. *Cross the road, and walk left to a stile and Public Footpath sign on the right. Cross the stile, then another, and bear right to a third stile behind two garages. Cross this and a well-used footpath, and continue in the*

Constructed in 1652, and fuelled by charcoal, it produced nearly 400 tons of pig iron each year. It is thought the furnace may be the oldest surviving example in Europe.   Worsbrough Village, whilst not far from the more sprawling urban developments to the north and south, has maintained its rural character . Its church is of Norman origin and has some interesting features, whilst the settlement itself probably dates from Anglo-Saxon times. The Edmunds Arms, whilst having no historical significance, is geared to the contemporary needs of families.

Refreshments Edmunds Arms in Worsbrough Village. Beer Garden. Red Lion, near Worsbrough Mill Car Park. Beer garden.

---

same direction alongside a row of bungalows, then a wall. The footpath ends at the road that goes through Worsbrough Village.

9. *Turn left into the village. Walk past the Edmunds Arms to Priory Close on the left. Part way along Priory Close, turn left at a Public Footpath sign. After only a few metres, turn right by a wall on the right- a yellow arrow marks the way. Continue along the descending footpath through arable fields to a stile. Cross the stile, turn right, then fork left almost immediately to go downhill to a stile at the main road. Cross the road, then a stile and continue back to the start.*

SHORTER VARIATIONS

I. As for 1 and 2 above, then, instead of turning right,
   (i) Go straight on along the track towards houses (Rockley Old Hall). Continue over a stile by a gate, cross a tarmac drive, and pass just right of the house to gain a stile. (ii) Cross the stile and fork left down to a gravel footpath, then go left to a footbridge. (iii) After crossing this, turn sharp right to a stile. Cross it, then go left and follow the stiled footpath to the A61. Cross the road and the stile opposite. Keep straight on up the field ahead, then climb stone steps to a stile. (iv) Cross the stile, turn left and continue to another stile, then follow the path to Priory Close (as mentioned in 9 above) . Continue as for 9 above to finish. (2½ miles)

II. *As for the above variation to the footbridge, then continue along the gravel footpath to a track. Cross the track to pick up the footpath going alongside the reservoir and back to the start. (2¼ miles)*

III. *Follow the footpath around the reservoir. (1½miles)*

Langsett Reservoir and Midhope Moor

Outline   Langsett - Upper Midhope ~ - Langsett Reservoir ~ Mickleden Edge ~ Langsett

Summary   A varied and picturesque reservoir walk just inside the Peak District National Park. Apart from the short section of road used to cross the Langsett Dam, footpaths and tracks are followed through a mixture of forest and open moorland. Any ascent is gradual, and much of the route is on the level. The shorter variation is suitable for younger children and a good introduction to moorland walking. After wet weather, make allowances for conditions underfoot.

Attractions   As with other reservoirs in this corner of South Yorkshire, Langsett Reservoir, with its forest surround, has enriched rather than spoiled the natural landscape. And for the child, the variety of forest, lake and moorland make for a stimulating and satisfying experience in the outdoors.

After crossing the dam you soon enter Upper Midhope, a tiny hamlet with abcient origins. From here, a forest track leads around the southern edge of the reservoir to North America! Apparently, during the Second World War , American troops were based here for a while. What you will find at North America are the ruins of a farmhouse which children will quickly convert into an adventure playground. Apart from this, it is situated at a particularly good vantage point above the reservoir and facing the dam. It is, in other words, a good excuse to stop for awhile, get your bearings and absorb the views. Also, the local sheep provide ready entertainment for all, since they are attracted like wasps to a jam jar should they sense the possibility of being offered morsels from your packed lunch.

If the longer walk is chosen, on leaving the ruin the footpath continues beyond the upper limit of the farm's abandoned fields with their still standing dry stone walls. The moors now stretch out as far as the eye can see, and lowland grasses give way to luxuriant heather growth, the territory of the red grouse. The footpath seems to be headed out into the wilderness but, instead, comes to an abrupt and dramatic conclusion at Mickleden Edge. This forms one side of a narrow, steep-sided and deep valley etched out by the meandering Mickleden Beck.

continued on page 28

Route 5

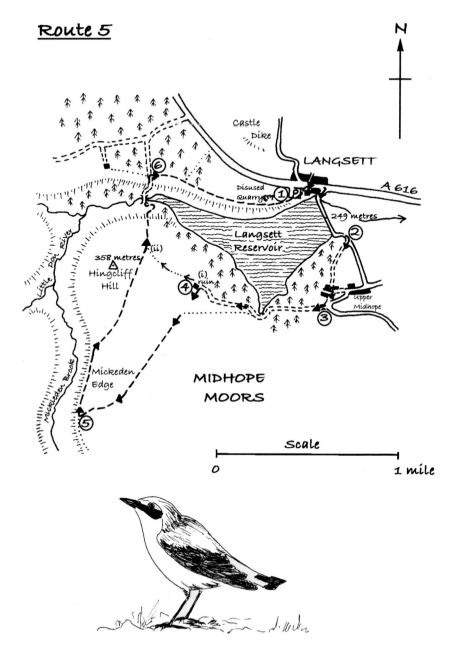

Scale

0   1 mile

Wheatear - summer visitor
(prominent white rump in flight)

Route 5

Langsett Reservoir and Midhope Moor   5 miles

(Shorter Variation 3½ miles)

START   *In Langsett Barn car park and picnic site, 150 metres up from the Waggon and Horses Public House. (GR 212005)*

ROUTE

1. *Leave the car park and walk back to and past the Waggon and Horses, then take the minor road on the right. Continue across the dam and uphill to a track on the right after a bend.*

2. *Turn right here and follow the track alongside a plantation, forking left before reaching buildings at Upper Midhope. Turn left at the cottages and, in a few metres, turn right and walk down a grassy track to reach the start of the forestry track that runs alongside the reservoir.*

3. *Follow the track around the southern edge of the reservoir to where it ends at a ruined farmhouse.*

4. *On arriving at a gate, turn left (do not go through it) and walk with a wall on the right. Continue along this to a T-junction of paths on Mickleden Edge.*

5. *Turn right and follow the path all the way down to and across a bridge over the Little Don. Continue uphill along a track as far as the way marked path leading right.*

6. *Follow the way marked path through the woodland back to Langsett Barn car park. (The quarry mentioned in the narrative is accessible from this path.)*

SHORTER VARIATION

As for 1 to 3 above to the ruin, then:

i. *Continue along the footpath in the same direction to a T -junction of footpaths.*

ii. *Turn right here and join 3 before the bridge across the Little Don.*

The route followed from here back down to the reservoir is an ancient 'road' known as Cut Gate, which linked Penistone to Upper Derwent. 'Gata' is Old Norse for path or passage. The location of an Iron Age settlement at Castle Dike near Langsett, however, suggests this was probably a trade route long before the Nordic settlers arrived.

On the way back along the northern edge of the reservoir, the footpath cuts through pine forest. Near the end of the walk a secluded quarry is passed. With a shallow pool at its foot colonised by frogs, the place is also of botanical interest and is well worth exploration.

Refreshments Waggon and Horses at Langsett. Cafe in Langsett.

Cannon Hall Country Park

Route 6   **4¼ miles**

(Shorter Variations 2¼ & 3 miles)

Green Moor and Upper Don Valley

Outline   Wortley Top Forge ~ Tin Mill Dam ~ Green Moor ~ Wortley Top Forge

Summary   This walk shares the start with the next one, and the two could be combined to provide a longer distance walk for a fit party. The area explored by this route is to the west of the River Don, which has a very Pennine flavour and contrasts sharply with the more gently rolling countryside to the east of the river. Although the first half mile is easy walking, the following half mile to the top of a ridge is, in parts, steep and quite strenuous. However, the views are rewarding, and the remainder of the walk is on the level or downhill. The tracks and footpaths used are mostly well-defined, and the last half mile is along a quiet country lane.

Attractions The walk starts in the picturesque setting of the Upper Don Valley just across the river from Wortley Top Forge. This is an industrial museum in the process of being restored and is well worth a visit. Its history is briefly described in the notes for Route 7. Let it suffice to say at this point that it has a little tea-shop, which makes it an even more attractive proposition after a walk.

About half a mile from the start, a lovely part of the Don Valley is entered, where the river is crossed by a footbridge or, if preferred, some ancient stepping stones. The steep wooded hillside of Tin Mill Rocher rises above what was once the river's floodplain and upon which is situated Tin Mill Dam. This used to be a mill pond but is now an angler's preserve, as is the stretch of river in this vicinity. This is a pity, since the youngster keen on birdwatching is denied access to the very place where he or she is likely to see less commonly sighted species such as yellow wagtail and dipper.

After the steep climb out of the valley, the top of an exposed ridge is reached. A little further on is Green Moor delf. An overgrown and long disused quarry, the place is ideal for play and exploration. Since the delf was abandoned, it has become colonised by an interesting variety of wild plants, which includes goat-willow, hoary alison, rowan, broom, gorse, heather and bilberry. The stone that was quarried here was known as 'Green Moor Delph'. From the quarry, it was taken by horse and cart to Worsbrough Bridge for movement by boat and to Wortley Station. A fine buildingstone, Green Moor Delph was sent to all parts of the country. It was also popular as a flagstone, and the paving stones around Sheffield

continued on page 32

29

Route 6

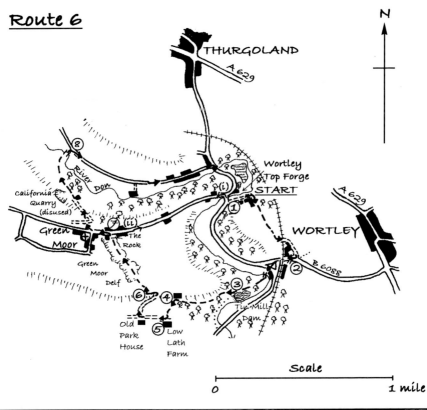

The River at Bradfield

Route 6

Green Moor and Upper Don Valley   4¼ miles

(Shorter Variations 2 & 3 miles)

START   *Adjacent to Wortley Top Forge Museum. The museum is signposted at Wortley and Thurgoland and is situated to the west of the A629. Park on the opposite side of the river to the museum at the start of a track. (G.R. 294997)*

ROUTE

1. *From the car park walk up the track. This bends right past a row of cottages, continues along the edge of a field, then crosses a bridge over a disused railway. Follow the continuation of the track past farm buildings to reach a road (86088).*

2. *Turn right and walk under the railway bridge. Turn left immediately, then cross over to a Public Footpath sign. Continue down to a minor road on the opposite side of which is a row of terraced houses. Go through a gate on the right of the houses. Carry on over a footbridge and follow the wide bridlepath, which bears right then left in a few metres. Continue along the wide bridlepath, passing Tin Mill Dam on the left, to where a prominent footpath forks up to the right through woods.*

3. *Take this footpath, which climbs steeply through the woods. Keeping straight on, and ignoring any other possibilities, continue to a stile in the wall at the top edge of the wood.*

4. *Turn left after the stile and follow a track down to a gate. Continue along the way marked footpath, which avoids a boggy area before arriving in a farmyard.*

5. *Turn right to follow a farm track to another farm (Old Park House). Pass the farm on the right, then turn sharp right up a track leading steeply uphill.*

6. *At the top of the steep hill, turn left off the track and walk with a wall on your right to reach a stile next to a gate on the right. Cross the stile and follow the wall on the right to a stone stile. Cross this, then bear left to reach a stepping stile set in a high wall. After climbing over the stile, go right along a well-used footpath through Green Moor Delf, an overgrown quarry Continue to The Rock (a pub) and a minor road.*

7. *Turn left at the road and walk to the Public Footpath sign and stile opposite the Methodist Church. Cross the stile and bear left downhill to a track. Turn right and follow the track, which bends in a hairpin down to the left and continues to Trunce Farm. Continue past the farm along a disused section of the track (California Quarry is up on the left) , which*

31

City Hall are from Green Moor. Quarrying ceased in 1936 with the introduction of concrete.

The village of Green Moor, perched high above the Don, has several interesting buildings. In the entrance to the quarry is the appropriately named public house 'The Rock'. Next to it is a small building within which is the old village water pump, which was used until 1951, when a piped water supply was brought to Green Moor. Further up the road is the village school. Built in 1936, an interesting feature is that the headteacher's house is an integral part of the building.

On the way back down to the river and valley, California Quarry is passed. This is worth a short diversion to view the abundance of flowerless plants that have taken root here, a sign of the clean air hereabouts. Several types of lichen grow on the stones and wood, and various fungi thrive in the damp and sheltered surrounds of the disused quarry.

After crossing the River Don the way back is along Old Mill Lane. On the right, New Mill is passed. Still manufacturing wire, the mill was once owned by relatives of William Wordsworth.

Refreshments   The Rock at Green Moor. Beer garden.
Tea-shop at Wortley Top Forge.

---

eventually stops at a gate with a stile. Cross the stile and continue along a field footpath in the same direction to pick up a footpath heading downhill towards the river. Follow this over a footbridge and up to a lane.

8.   *Turn right and follow the lane to a T -junction. Turn right, cross a bridge and walk back to the start, passing Wortley Top Forge en route.*

SHORTER VARIATIONS

i.   *From the car park return to the road. Turn right and cross the bridge, then turn left up a minor road that leads directly to Green Moor. Continue from Green Moor as for 7 and 8 above. (2¼ miles)*

ii.   *As for 1 to 6 above to The Rock at Green Moor, then turn right and walk down the minor road back to the start. (3 Miles)*

Mill Moor, Hermit Hill and Wortley Park

Outline Wortley Top Forge ∼ Mill Moor Height ∼ Crane Moor ∼ Hermit Hill ∼Buck Park ∼Wortley Top Forge

Summary Starting by the River Don near Wortley Top Forge, the walk soon climbs out of the valley and weaves its way across the attractive rolling countryside east of the Don, passing through farmland, the picturesque parkland surrounding Wortley Hall, and wilder tracts of woodland. A combination of tracks and footpaths are followed, short sections of some of the field footpaths being ill-defined but well-stiled. On a clear day the views are particularly good from several points on the walk.

Attractions The start of the walk is just across the river from Wortley Top Forge, an industrial museum in the process of being restored. The present ironworks was built in 1727 and continued to operate unti11910, its last fifty years or so in the manufacture of railway axles. There was, however, a bloomery on the site in Elizabethan times, and in 1638 two forges existed. The ironworks boasts the only example of an 18th century water-powered hammer set in a forge. In addition, there is a fine display of working engines, a recreated 19th century workshop, a tea-shop and miniature steam railway into the bargain - which is a good reason for postponing a visit until after the walk!

A little way on from the forge, the walk follows a quiet stretch of the River Don. With a bit of patience and luck, you may be treated to a sighting of a kingfisher, whose vivid plumage is unmistakable. Grey wagtail, and occasionally yellow wagtail, also may be seen along this section.

Leaving the natural vegetation of the river banks, it is interesting to observe the variety in land use on the journey to Crane Moor. The steep valley slope rising from the Don, with its heavier, wet clay soils, is used for rough grazing. The short, steep strip above the main road rising to Mill Moor Height is uneconomical to farm and has been left to its own devices, producing beech woodland. The very top of the broad, rounded ridge, where soils are well drained and which gets a maximum of sunlight, is devoted to arable farming. And the more gentle lower slopes of the other side of the ridge are given over to pasture land mainly for dairy farming.

continued on page 36

Route 7

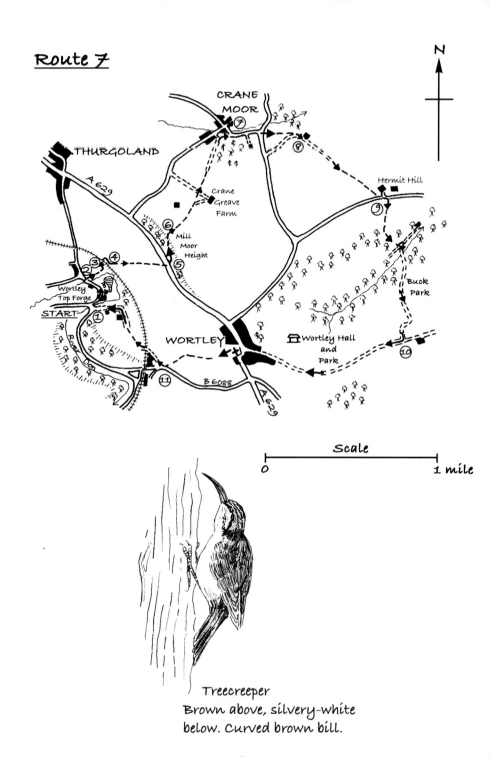

N

CRANE MOOR

THURGOLAND

A 629

Crane Greave Farm

Mill Moor Height

Hermit Hill

Wortley Top Forge

START

Buck Park

WORTLEY

Wortley Hall and Park

B 6088

A 629

River Don

Scale

0   1 mile

Treecreeper
Brown above, silvery-white
below. Curved brown bill.

Route 7

Mill Moor, Hermit Hill and Wortley Park   5½ miles

START   *Adjacent to Wortley Top Forge Museum, as for Route 6.*

ROUTE

1. *From the car park, go back to the road and turn right. and continue past the museum along the pavement. In about ¼ mile, a second road bridge is reached.*

2. *Cross this, then turn right at the Public Footpath sign. Follow the riverside footpath for a short distance till it forks. Take the left fork and follow it for about 100 metres only. After this, the footpath is forced to the right alongside the river, since a railway embankment lies straight ahead. The next objective is a pedestrian subway that goes through the embankment further left.*

3. *Bear left, therefore, and head for a gap in the hawthorns. A fence running more or less parallel to the railway embankment is reached. Between the two, a narrow footpath leads up to the pedestrian subway. Go through it, turn right on the other side and walk to a stile on the left made from railway sleepers.*

4. *Cross this stile, then bear half right up the field ahead (no footpath in evidence), the objective being a stone stile in the top right-hand corner of the field.*

5. *Cross the stile and the main road (A629) to a Public Footpath sign a short distance to the left. Follow a grassy track up through a wood, ignoring a well-used footpath that crosses the track. Continue to a gateway and field at the top edge of the wood.*

6. *The right of way departs at right angles to the upper perimeter of the wood, although the footpath has been ploughed. Follow the direction of the right of way to a wooden stile that is concealed by the lie of the land to begin with. Cross the stile and carry on in the same direction down through pasture to another stile. Cross this, then bear slightly right to the corner of a field ahead fenced with barbed wire. Just to the right of it is a farm (Crane Greave). Continue alongside the fence, keeping the farm on the right, then cross a track to gain a stile. Cross this and continue straight ahead until a track is reached on the left of a wood. Follow the track, turning right at the bottom edge of the wood, and continue to a minor road in Crane Moor (The Rock Inn is to the left).*

In a little valley between Crane Moor and Wortley the walk passes through picturesque woodland. This supports a variety of wildflowers, amongst which cuckoo flower and broad-leaved willow herb may be found, as well as a host of other species.

On climbing out of the valley a track is followed through Wortley Park which, with its hall, is reminiscent of Chatsworth in Derbyshire. Although the present hall dates mainly from 1743, in the first decade of the 16th century Sir Thomas Wortley built the first of the family's halls on the site. It was he who laid out the park. In the process, he ruthlessly destroyed farms and settlements in order to achieve his ends. The village of Wortley was already a settlement back in 1250 and was on the medieval salt trail from Cheshire to Rotherham and the market towns further east.

Refreshments   Rock Inn at Crane Moor. Beer Garden.
                     Wortley Arms at Wortley. Beer garden.

———————

7. *Turn right and walk along the road to a T -junction. Go straight across to a stile (Public Footpath sign), then continue in the same direction up the field ahead, aiming for a silage store comes into view, and crossing another stile on the way.*

8. *On reaching a farm track, follow it past the farm immediately ahead and continue along this to where it ends at agate and stile. Cross the stile, then go up steeply to another stile on the skyline. After crossing this, carry on in the same direction. After reaching a hedge, keep it on the left and go straight on to reach a minor road at Stone Farm.*

9. *Turn left at the road. Walk past the farm to a Public Footpath sign and stile on the right. Cross the stile and follow the footpath alongside the hedge down to a wood. Follow the footpath through the wood to where it ends at a gravel track. Cross this and continue along another track leading uphill through the wood. Fllow the track to the edge of the wood, then bear half right along a path across a large field to reach a track. Turn right and follow this track to Wortley (I mile) . Turn right at the main road, then left by the church boundary wall at a Public Footpath sign. After a gateway, a paved footpath is followed downhill through fields to a road.*

10. *A track coming from the right joins the road at the same point. Turn sharp right to follow the track behind buildings. Go over a railway bridge, then bear right along a path that leads back to the start.*

Bolsterstone and Whitwell Moor

Outline   Underbank   Reservoir~   Stone   Moor   ~   Bolsterstone   ~ Whitwell Moor ~ Underbank Reservoir.

Summary   A walk with plenty of variety and historical interest. Virtually all the uphill walking is in the first two miles, and much of this gradual. On reaching Bolsterstone, a hilltop stronghold in ancient times, a ridge is followed westwards from which there are excellent views. Here a stretch of moorland is crossed before a descent through pastures leads back down into Stocksbridge. Apart from a few short sections of road- walking, the route follows a mixture of tracks and well defined footpaths.

Attractions From Stocksbridge, a steep, abandoned old farm track leads uphill to the farms and pasture land overlooking the town and, eventually, to the very attractive little village of Bolsterstone. Its name is a corruption of 'Walderston', meaning the village whose chieftain was Walder. Situated on the crest of a ridge, in Saxon times the settlement was a stronghold. Half a mile east of the village is Walder's Low, the Saxon word 'hlaw' meaning a heaped structure and usually denoting a burial mound. In medieval times an important building of some kind existed on the site of the present village. Above an old iron-studded door next to the remains of an archway on the opposite side of the square to the church is an inscription: 'Porter's Lodge, Bolsterstone Castle. Supposed date of doorway A.D. 1250'. Although it is unlikely there was ever a Norman Castle on this site, local historian Jack Branston, in his book 'History of Stocksbridge', provides evidence for the existence of a medieval hall. A further clue to the village 's importance as an administrative centre in the past is the existence of the stocks, situated next to the church.

Walking west from the village, the ridge is followed to its highest point, this whole section overlooking Broom head Reservoir. From the triangulation point, the views are splendid in most directions. It is also a superb spot for the packed lunch, for nearby is a strip of woodland well suited to exploration and play. The woodland stretches for about half a mile. The more natural vegetation bordering the wood is a mixture of heather, cotton grass, bilberry and bracken and the occasional rowan. These provide a habitat and cover for wheatear, stonechat, meadow pipit and skylark.

continued on page 40

Route 8

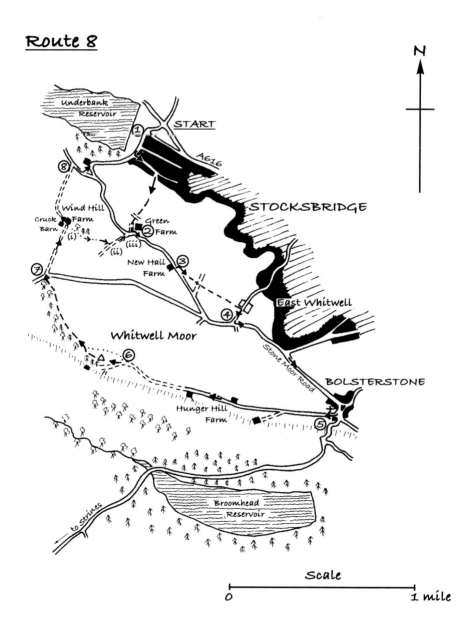

N

Underbank Reservoir

START

①

A616

STOCKSBRIDGE

⑧

Wind Hill Farm

Cruck Barn

Green Farm

②

(i)

(iii)

(ii)

New Hall Farm

③

④

East Whitwell

⑦

Whitwell Moor

⑥

Stone Moor Road

BOLSTERSTONE

Hunger Hill Farm

⑤

to Strines

Broomhead Reservoir

Scale

0   1 mile

Route 8
Bolsterstone and Whitwell Moor

5 miles

(Shorter Variation 4 miles)

START *Leave the A616 Stocksbridge By-Pass by the west exit to Stocksbridge, then turn right into a cul-de-sac and park adjacent to the dam. GR 254995.*

ROUTE

1. *Walk across the dam then turn left into Smithy Moor Lane. Turn right and continue uphill to Cross Lane. Walk up Cross Lane to Green Lane on the right. Continue up Green Lane then straight on up the footpath that is all that remains of an old walled track. Where the farm track is reached-Green Farm is just to the left- go straight across and continue to a country lane.*

2. *Turn left at the lane and continue to a stile and Public Footpath sign on the left and opposite New Hall Farm.*

3. *Cross the stile and another a few metres on, then continue along a field footpath, keeping a wall on the left. Cross a track and continue along the footpath to a minor road.*

4. *Turn right along the road and walk up to a T -junction. Turn left and follow the roadside, then a pavement, to Bolsterstone (about 2/3 mile).*

5. *In Bolsterstone, turn right at the lane which separates the former village school from the church graveyard. Follow this to where it becomes a track at a gate (cottage on the left). Cross a stile on the right of the gate and continue along the track in the same direction. Where it bends downhill to the left a footpath leads straight on along the ridge.*

6. *Follow the footpath, forking left to reach the triangulation pillar (clearly visible). The more well-used footpath skirts around to the right of the highest point. Continue past the triangulation pillar and take one of the gaps in the wall on the right, where the main footpath can be rejoined. Continue in the same direction with the wall on the left alongside the top of a wood. The footpath eventually meets a country lane.*

7. *Cross the lane and continue downhill along a track (Public Footpath sign) to a gateway on the left. Go through this, then another gateway at Wind Hill Farm (Cruck barn on left). Continue along the farm track down to a lane.*

8. *Turn right along the lane, and walk to a stile on the left in 150 metres. Cross the stile and, keeping a wall on the left, go down to a stile and minor road. Continue downhill along the road back to the start.*

Soon after dropping down from the ridge, the skeleton of a cruck barn can be examined at close quarters at Wind Hill Farm. Its present state provides an ideal opportunity for studying how such timber-framed barns were constructed. The southern end of the building now containing the farmhouse is also a cruck structure.

Refreshments Castle Inn at Bolsterstone.

SHORTER VARIATION

Park on Stone Moor Road near Bolsterstone. Continue as for 5 Wind Hill Farm, then:

i.   *Turn right and, keeping a wall on the left, follow the stiled footpath to a track.*

ii. *Turn left at the track and walk down to a minor road.*

iii. *Go straight on and follow the road past Green Farm. Continue to the stile and Public Footpath sign mentioned in 2 above, then as for 3 and 4 to finish.*

Local Inhabitants, Burbage Valley

Route 9

6 miles

(Shorter Variations 4¾ & 4 miles)

Spout House Hill and Hollin Edge Height

Outline   More Hall Reservoir~ Brightholmlee ~ Spout House Hill ~ Ewden ~ Bolsterstone ~ Hollin Edge Height ~ More Hall Reservoir

Summary   One of the more strenuous walks in this guide, taking in the high ground both north and south of More Hall Reservoir. There is a lot of interest en route and, on a clear day, there are splendid views of the surrounding hills and valleys. Although at the start of the walk about ¼ mile is alongside a main road - on a pavement - the remainder is along footpaths, tracks and quiet country lanes. The walk is not suitable for smaller children because of the hill walking involved.

Attractions In several places along the walk there is an air of remoteness, even though roads are never far away. And since some of the rights of way are little used, the walk presents more of a challenge than others in this guide! However, all the stiles are in place, no way is barred, and with a little concentration and attention to detail, the route will unfold.

From More Hall Reservoir a steady climb leads to the quaint old hamlet of Brightholmlee, with its 17th and 18th century farmhouses and cottages. A country lane, then field footpaths and tracks lead up steeply from Brightholmlee to the summit of Spout House Hill. There are old quarry workings here which are safe to explore and provide a good excuse to stop for a rest. The stone that was quarried here is known as millstone grit, used as a grind stone in the 18th and 19th century cutlery industry in Sheffield. The stone was also widely used as a building stone before the widespread introduction of brick.

A descent through picturesque countryside takes you to the village of Ewden, which is mostly a waterworks complex situated between Broom Head and More Hall Reservoirs. In contrast to the latter-day buildings, the stone architecture that forms part of the Broomhead Dam is much more in keeping with the surroundings.

A steep climb from Ewden leads to Bolsterstone, a village worth exploring whose history is briefly described in the notes for the previous walk. On leaving the village, the way back is mostly on the level or downhill. In other words, the hard work is over with, and you can relax and enjoy the extensive views across to the higher moorland in the west and the hilly country both north and south of the reservoirs. The descent from this lofty'

continued overleaf

41

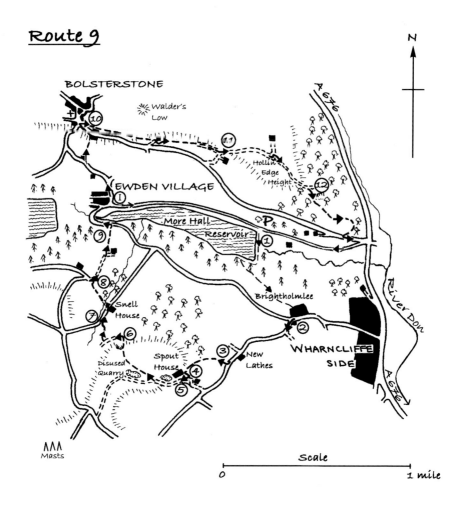

ridge is along old farm tracks and footpaths that pass through natural woodland of oak, rowan and holly. If the walk is to be done in autumn, take containers, for unpolluted blackberries grow in profusion along parts of this last section.

Refreshments   Castle Inn at Bolsterstone.

Route 9

Spout House Hill and Hollin Edge Height   6 miles
(Shorter Variations 4¾ & 4 miles)

START   *Turn west off the A616 a quarter of a mile north of Wharncliffe Side towards Ewden and More Hall Reservoir (the Yorkshire Water entrance to the South Yorkshire Sailing Club). Park adjacent to the dam. GR287958.*

ROUTE

1. *Cross the dam along the walkway and continue along the far side of the reservoir for a short distance. Take the path that doubles back uphill to the left. Continue via two stiles then follow a track up into Brightholmlee.*

2. *Turn right, then left up the road signposted to Bradfield. Follow this uphill for just under half a mile to a stile and Public Footpath sign on the right just beyond a house on the left.*

3. *Cross the stile and follow the wall on the right up to another stile. Cross this, then bear left to gain stile.*

4. *Cross it and turn left along a grassy, walled track. Just before a farm building, turn left and go down and over another stile to gain a gravel track.*

5. *Turn right and follow the track uphill through two gates. Spout House Farm is up on the right. From the second gate, continue along the track, passing left of old quarry workings, for about 200 metres only, at which point the track cuts through higher ground. At the end of the cutting, bear right off the track by a wall that marks the right-hand boundary of more old quarry workings further along. Walk on the right of the wall to pick up an old disused trench like track and follow this to a stone stepping stile on the right of a gate. Cross the stile and bear right downhill to a track, passing further quarry workings.*

6. *Go left along the track to gateposts, then turn right and go straight down to the bottom right-hand corner of the field to a stile and country lane.*

7. *Turn right and walk down the lane as far as an old farm building on the right (Snell House). Opposite this, on the left, though easily missed, is a footpath which descends wooden steps. Follow the footpath down and across a footbridge over a ravine, then go up to a stile. Cross it and bear right across a field to another stile. Continue over this and downhill in the same direction to a stile and tarmac track.*

8. *Turn right and go downhill along the track to a way-marked stile in the wall on the left just before the track bends to the right. Cross the stile and continue*

downhill and over several stiles, keeping close to the stream on the left, to a road.

9. *Turn left. Follow the road around the top of More Hall Reservoir, then continue uphill towards Bolsterstone; Fork right along a Public Footpath (signposted) that passes right of Castlearmstrong. Follow the stiled footpath steeply up to a road. Turn left and follow the road to a T-junction in Bolsterstone.*

10. *On the immediate right is a stile and Public Footpath sign. Turn right here and follow the footpath to a renovated farmhouse. Follow the path behind the house and over stiles, then follow the stiled footpath to a gate and a strip of woodland. Follow a track through the wood to a T-junction of tracks.*

11. *Turn left and continue uphill along a track. Just after it turns sharp left towards a farm, turn right along a less well-used track (Public Footpath sign). After going through a wood, the track stops abruptly. A few metres before it reaches this point, a footpath forks off downhill to the right.*

12. *Follow this down through woods. Keep straight on, ignoring a path going left to a shooting range. On emerging from the woods, keep to the wall on the right and continue down to a road. Turn left, then sharp right along the reservoir road to finish.*

SHORTER VARIATIONS

i. *As for 1 to 9 above as far as the reservoir, then turn right and follow the road back to the dam. (4.75 miles)*

ii. *Follow the road alongside the reservoir to Ewden Village, then continue as for 9 to 12 above. (4 miles)*

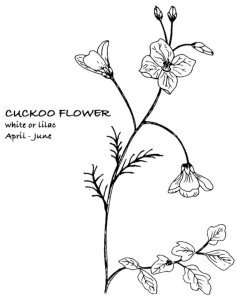

CUCKOO FLOWER
white or lilac
April - June

Bradfield Dale and Dale Dyke Reservoir

Outline Low Bradfield ~ Brogging ~ Hall field ~ Annet Bridge ~ Low Bradfield

Summary A combination of tracks, footpaths and country lanes are used in a picturesque excursion around the infamous Dale Dike Reservoir. Whilst at most times, the sections of country lane used in the walk see little traffic, on summer Sundays some motorised sightseers have to be reckoned with.

Attractions Getting started on the walk proper can be like running the gauntlet for parents. The car park is situated next to the village playground. And about 200 metres further on, the children are again lured away from the main objective of the outing by a delightful riverside play and picnic area in the village. Whilst the children are otherwise occupied, it is worth perusing the immediate surroundings. An obvious feature of Low Bradfield is the very large village green. In Anglo-Saxon times this was pasture land, and the settlement took its name from this broad field or 'brad feld'. Up on the hill is High Bradfield, originally known as Kirk Town, the town or hamlet with a church. Sited just east of a motte-and-bailey castle on Bailey Hill is Bradfield Church. The original church was Norman but was rebuilt in the Late Middle Ages.

On leaving the village, the walk leads through the part of Bradfield Dale not occupied by reservoirs. Chaffinch, pied wagtail and wren are commonly seen hereabouts amongst the sparse cover provided by black thorn, hazel and silver birch. Further on, the footpath passes through plantation that borders Dale Dike Reservoir. This is a mixture of spruce, scots pine and larch, although oak and sycamore grow alongside the tracks and in clearings. Keep an eye out for tree-creeper and goldcrest on the pines.

After coming out of the forest, the footpath crosses a stream that has carved a ravine into the steep ground. Across it, a log has fallen that children find irresistible to test out their daring. Not far from this pleasant spot is Strines Dam, at one end of which is Brogging House with its roaming turkeys, bantam cockerels and various other species of domestic poultry. The walk back along the west side of Dale Dike Reservoir is via an old track that goes parallel to the reservoir but about 150 feet above it, so that there of the original Dale Dike Dam. Although the cause of the collapse was disputed, subsidence within the dam, combined with a strong west wind pushing a great weight of water against it, seem to have been responsible are good open views both across and down the valley. Halfway along this track is the splendidly situated Hallfield Hall.

Looking down upon the reservoir and its dam from these peaceful

continued on page 48

45

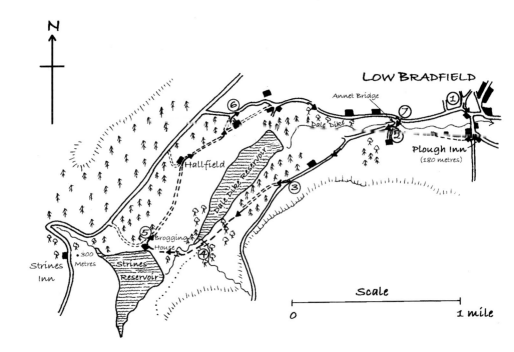

Route 10

Mill Pond, Worsbrough Mill

Route 10
Bradfield Dale and Dale Dike Reservoir   4½miles

START   *In Low Bradfield. The car park is situated next to the village playground. Take the Strines road (Fair House Lane), then the first road on the right (The Sands). (G.R. 262921)*

ROUTE

1. *From the car park, walk back down Fair House Lane and turn right along Mill Lee Road. Continue as far as The Plough on the left. Almost immediately opposite on the right is a track and Public Footpath sign. Follow this track to where it ends at a stile. Continue straight on along a footpath above the stream to where it meets a lane just left of a bridge (Annet Bridge).*

2. *Turn left and follow the lane uphill, passing a cottage on the right, to a stile and Public Footpath sign on the right.*

3. *Cross the stile and continue along a forest track to where it ends at a stone stepping stile. Continue in the same direction along the way- marked footpath across sheep pasture.*

4. *After crossing a stream continue to a stile on the right. Continue along the footpath, then across a wooden bridge and go up beside Strines Dam to cottage and a track. The cottage is Brogging House.*

5. *Turn right along the track and follow this for about a mile to a junction with a country lane. This includes a short waymarked diversion around round Hallfield.*

6. *Turn right and walk down the winding lane for a mile, passing the Haychatters Inn on the way, to where a lane joins from the right.*

7. *Turn sharp right here and continue over a bridge (Annet Bridge) to a stile on the left crossed on the outward journey. Turn left here and retrace your steps back to the start.*

surroundings, it is hard to imagine the devastation caused by the collapse for the destruction and loss of life of that fateful night of March 11,1864. The raging torrent that swept down the Loxley and Don Valleys, as well as flattening farms, houses and mills, left a death toll of around 250, whilst hundreds more were made homeless or left without employment. A sobering thought as you head for the Haychatters Inn en route back to Low Bradfield.

Refreshments The Plough at Low Bradfield. Pleasant beer garden.

The Church at Silkstone

Loxley Valley

Outline   Loxley ~ Rowel Bridge ~ Storrs ~ Stacey Bank - Rowel Bridge~ Loxley

Summary   A fine walk in and around a valley that evokes a strong atmosphere of Sheffield's industrial past. Starting at Loxley, the walk passes through riverside woodland before climbing steeply out of the valley and on to the high pasture land to the south. From here, there are extensive views of the valley and the hills beyond. After half a mile of walking along a quiet country lane, a descent is made to Stacey Bridge below Damflask Dam. The last two miles follow the riverside back to the start, passing interesting relics of past water-powered industries. A leaflet, entitled 'Loxley Valley Walk' and produced as part of a joint Sheffield City Council and Countryside Commission project, describes a longer route that starts at Malin Bridge. The leaflet also contains a lot of information about the valley's industrial past and its natural history.

Attractions   Near the start of the walk, the River Loxley is crossed next to Little Matlock Rolling Mills where the largest surviving water-wheel in the area can be seen. With the workers' cottages nearby, it is interesting to imagine how the scene would have looked a century or so ago.

Across the river, a footpath takes you through attractive woodland of beech, oak and elm, although much of the elm is affected by Dutch Elm disease. Beyond the woods, an area of uncultivated grassland is encountered, where hawthorn and a variety of wildflowers thrive. In the summer months, feeding on the insects which themselves live on the wildflowers, blackcap and whitethroat may be sighted as well as more commonly seen species.

At Rowel Bridge two water-wheels once powered grinding workshops similar to that known as Shepherd's Wheel on Porter Brook. However, only the wheel pits survive. From here, a steep climb through woods, then an area of scrub, leads abruptly to the wide open space of hill pastures, and for the next mile or so the views of the countryside around the Loxley Valley are uninterrupted,

The way back down to the river is alongside a meandering fast-flowing stream. This is particularly pleasant and would be an ideal spot to pause and let the youngsters play a while. Amongst the hedgerows in the vicinity yellowhammer, linnet and wren may be seen.

continued on page 52

Route 11

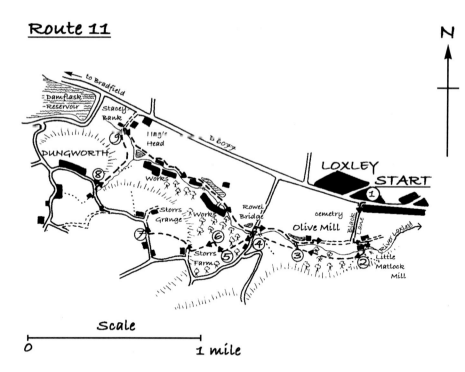

N

Scale

0   1 mile

Footbridge across Wyming Brook

Route 11
Loxley Valley

4½miles

Shorter Variations 2¾ & 1¼miles

START *Park on Loxley Road (B6077) about a mile west of Malin Bridge and on the town side of Loxley Cemetery. The walk starts down Black Lane, which runs alongside the cemetery and is signposted to Little Matlock Rolling Mills. (G.R. 309898)*

ROUTE

1. *Walk down Black Lane towards the river. Turn left at the fork and continue to Little Matlock Rolling Mills on the right. Cross the river by footbridges on the immediate left of the mill.*

2. *After crossing the river, take a right fork through woodland along a renovated and clearly defined footpath that stays well above the river but keeps more or less parallel to it. Go as far as a footpath sign (this was incorrect at the time of publication) .*

3. *Take the left fork at this point (do not cross the river) and continue to a stile. Cross this and make for Rowel Bridge as signposted. Continue across an old stone footbridge to gain the road at Rowel Bridge. T*

4. *Turn left and go across the bridge to a stile and Public Footpath sign on the right. Cross the stile and follow the fork signposted to Storrs Farm. After a climb, a stile is reached. Continue straight on with a wall on the right for 200 metres to the top corner of the second field on the right.*

5. *Turn right at this point and, keeping a wall on the left now, continue to and over a stone stile, then straight on to a signpost.*

6. *Turn left and continue along the way marked path to the hamlet. Turn sharp right, continue past a farm shed and cross a stile. Bear left to follow the path to Storrs Green. Continue to a lane.*

7. *Turn right at the lane (Storrs Carr) and follow it for just under ½ mile, first on the level, then downhill to where there is a cottage up a track on the left. Continue along the road, now uphill for 100 metres only to a stile*

   and Public Footpath sign on the right next to a cottage.

8. *Go right here. Stay on the footpath on the left of the stream, ignoring a more obvious looking right fork. Continue to a stone stile, then straight on to a signpost in the field ahead. Turn left to follow the sign for Damflask.*

From Stacey Bridge, where a short diversion could be made to the Nags Head for refreshment, the remainder of the walk is mainly by the riverside, with short diversions through mill yards. Next to the river are various channels, goits and dams which are relics of water-powered industries. These include grinding, forging, wire and rolling mills, corn mills, paper manufacture and clay-crushing for the refractories. The relics are mainly late 19th century, since the raging torrent that swept down the Loxley Valley following the collapse of the Dale Dike Dam in 1864 wiped out most of the earlier factories, mills and houses.

Although other mill ponds in the valley are maintained for angling, Rowel Bridge Dam has been so long abandoned that the process of colonisation by plants is well advanced. In addition to reeds and sedges, this wetland supports alders and willows. Such areas, known as 'carrs' in turn provide a habitat for various species of birds. In the summer months, willow warblers are regularly seen here.

Refreshments   Nags Head at Stacey Bridge.

---

9. *After crossing a stile, cross the river by a footbridge, then turn right along the footpath signposted to Rowel Bridge. (For the Nags Head, go straight on after the footbridge up the lane, then retrace your steps.) The walk back is well marked, the path staying close to the river except for signposted diversions around sections of the works. Continue to Rowel Bridge.*

10. *At Rowel Bridge, go left, then right along the way-marked footpath to Olive Dam. Leave the riverside for a track that starts at the entrance to Blakeley Marquees. Turn left up Black Lane to finish.*

SHORTER VARIATIONS

i. *Start at Rowel Bridge Picnic Area, ½ mile south of the B6077, on the Stannington- Dungworth road. Walk across the bridge, then as for 4 to 9 above. (2¾ miles)*

ii. *This takes the short section of the river between Rowel Bridge and then as for 1 to 3 Little Matlock. As for 10 above as far as Black Lane, above. (1¼ miles)*

Rivelin Valley

Outline   Rivelin Dams ~ Wyming Brook ~ Hallam Moor ~ Rivelin Dams

Summary   An excellent walk for children amidst the forest and moorland of the Upper Rivelin Valley, and situated within the Peak District National Park. There is lots of interest en route, and from the highest point on the walk there are especially fine views over the reservoirs and down the Rivelin Valley. Footpaths and forest tracks are followed throughout. After a spell of wet weather, the footpath alongside Wyming Brook becomes muddy in its lower section, and slippery stones may have to be reckoned with in parts.

Attractions   The walk begins at an attractive location beside the lower of the two Rivelin Dams. From here, a winding footpath is followed up the steep wooded valley etched out by Wyming Brook. Since it faces north, the valley has rather a dank and dewy atmosphere, and with its moss covered boulders, its tall pines, its tumbling stream and its little wooden bridges, the whole effect is quite enchanting.

On leaving Wyming Brook, a high level footpath along the forest moorland divide leads to a fine viewpoint overlooking the Rivelin Valley and its reservoirs. This is also a choice spot for a picnic but youngsters should be closely supervised, since the viewpoint is atop a 20 feet high outcrop of gritstone. Further on, and right alongside the footpath, a number of unusually shaped and dwarfish scots pines provide scope for exercise for the agile members of the party. Such pauses are opportune for the keen birdwatcher. Amidst the moorland grasses, the bracken and the bilberry, meadow pipit, wheatear and woodcock may be sighted. On the pine trees, keep a look out for tree-creeper, goldcrest, nuthatch and long-tailed tit.

After descending to the forest track, another half mile of ascent takes you through vegetation that gradually transforms from plantation woodland, through scrub, to heather clad moor. The uniformity of the plant on this particular stretch of moorland is a clear indication that it is cultivated for grouse, which in turn are cultivated for the grouse shooters. Along this section, conveniently situated just where a rest or distraction is needed, are child-sized rocks highly suited to the aspiring young climber .

On coming down from the moor, the tree-lined River Rivelin, not more than a wide stream at this point, is followed for some distance along a

continued on page 56

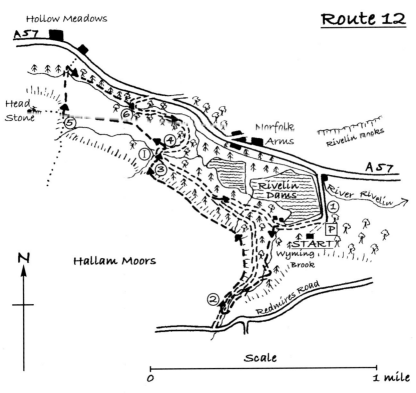

The Stocks at Green Moor

Route 12
Rivelin Valley

4 miles
(Shorter Variation 2½miles)

START *From the A57 Sheffield to Manchester road drive across the Rivelin Dam and park in Lower Rivelin car park. The road across the dam is not signposted but is open to traffic. (G.R. 273866)*

ROUTE

1. *From the car park follow the track alongside the reservoir for ¼ mile, then turn left opposite waterworks buildings. Follow the main footpath on the right of the stream. This bears slightly right uphill to begin with but soon bends left, after which it stays close by the stream and crosses it three times via wooden footbridges. Where the terrain levels out after coming out of the woods cross over the stream once more on stepping stones and go up to the track above the stream.*

2. *Turn left, then right in a few metres at a Public Footpath sign. Follow the footpath to the viewpoint overlooking the Rivelin Dams (partially obscured by trees). The path now bends to the left. Stay on the highest level footpath along the top edge of the wood, ignoring any footpaths bearing downhill to the right. Eventually, your path descends into a narrow valley, then bears right downhill to join a track.*

3. *Turn left and follow the track over a culvert, then up to a passing place on the left. A footpath joins here on the left.*

4. *Turn left and follow the footpath up on to the heather moor - the path forks but both converge a little way further on. Continue to a T -junction of footpaths (the prominent 'Headstone' is straight ahead at this point).*

5. *Turn right and continue downhill and across a footbridge over the River Rivelin. Turn right immediately after crossing the footbridge and follow the footpath alongside the stream to a bridge.*

6. *Turn right along the forest track. Follow this, then a left fork back to the start.*

SHORTER VARIATION

i. *As for I and 2 above, then turn right to continue as for 6 above.*

delightful little valley where there is ample opportunity for play and for picnicking. After leaving the riverside, the return journey is along forest tracks that descend gradually back to the starting point.

Refreshments None on the walk. Norfolk Arms on the A57 adjacent to the upper reservoir.

Burbage Bridge

Burbage Valley

Outline   Fox House ~ Carl Wark ~ Higger Tor ~Upper Burbage Bridge
~ Fox House

Summary   As with the Rivelin walk, this is especially good for children
because of the numerous opportunities to play and explore en route.
Starting at Fox House, the walk makes a tour of the rugged and craggy
moorland surrounding Burbage Brook. The first half is uphill in stages
along the west flank of the valley, whilst the second half of the walk is a
gradual descent along the east flank. Although well-defined footpaths can
be followed throughout, deviations to interesting features are mentioned in
the route description, and several options are given for the return leg of the
walk.

Attractions The walk starts in the grounds of Longshaw Estate, formerly a
shooting 'box' for the Dukes of Rutland but now more famous for its annual
sheepdog trials. On leaving the estate, the scenery changes abruptly from
cultivated parkland to the wild moorland of the Burbage Valley. Looking
from the road, the craggy summit of Carl Wark and, beyond it, Higger Tor
dominate the skyline.

   Carl Wark was an Iron Age fort, although the style of wall building on
its western perimeter suggests it was used as a fortification in the 5th or
6th century . The wall is of sturdy build and provides plenty of scope for
children wishing to test out their climbing skills.

   From Higger Tor, the highest point on the walk, there is a panoramic
view of the surrounding countryside. The prominent leaning block west of
its summit is worth exploring. Attaining a height of over 40 feet, the crack
up its fiercely overhanging south face was one of Joe Brown's conquests.
Forty years after its first ascent, the 'Rasp', as it is known to climbers, is still
considered to be a test piece for aspiring 'hard climbers'. Not far from the
leaning block, and more appropriate for pint-sized pioneers, is a tangled
cluster of fallen boulders ideal for scrambling over and squeezing beneath.

   About half a mile further on is Upper Burbage Bridge, the halfway
mark. From here, the way is downhill. The line of cliffs up on the left form
Burbage Edge. This is a very popular venue for novice climbers as well as
those using the rocks as an outdoor gymnasium to tone up body and mind
for difficult routes.

Continued on page 60

Route 13

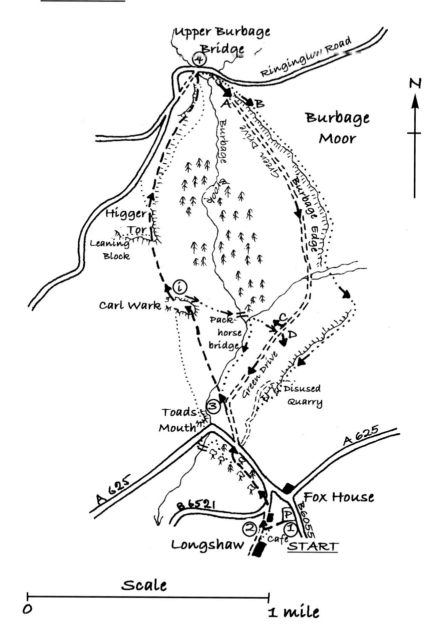

Upper Burbage Bridge

Ringinglow Road

④

A B

Burbage Moor

N

Burbage Brook

Green Drive

Burbage Edge

Higger Tor

Leaning Block

ⓘ

Carl Wark

Pack horse bridge

C

D

Green Drive

Disused Quarry

③

Toads Mouth

A 625

A 625

B 6521

Fox House

B 6055

Longshaw

②

P

①

cafe

START

Scale

0   1 mile

58

Route 13
Burbage Valley

4½miles

(Shorter Variation 2 1/2 miles)

START *At Longshaw Estate Car Park, about 200 metres south of the Fox House Inn on the B6055. (G.R. 267801)*

ROUTE

1. *From the car park, walk downhill along a footpath, forking right just before a footbridge, and gain the drive that leads to Longshaw House.*

2. *Turn right and follow the drive to the Lodge and the road (B6521). Cross the road and the stile opposite. Continue along a footpath, forking right to a stile and the main road (A625) in about 1/4 mile. Cross the road to pick up a track (known as Green Drive). Go through a handgate and continue along the track to where it bends after gateposts.*

3. *Fork left off the track at this point and follow a footpath down to and across Burbage Brook, then continue uphill to Carl Wark. Once at the summit, bear left to the western perimeter wall of the hill-fort and make an exit in the northwest corner. The footpath descends a little before heading uphill to Higger Tor. Follow the path up on to the summit. (To get to the leaning block, walk left along the top of the crags for about 200 metres, then scramble down amongst boulders to get below it. Find the summit footpath again to continue the walk.) From the summit, keep straight on in the same direction, ignoring a left fork down to a minor road. The footpath ends at a stile and the road at Upper Burbage Bridge.*

4. *Either cross the stile and turn right to gain a handgate on the far side of the bridge or cross the two streams immediately below the road to gain the track (Green Drive) on the other side of the valley. There are several options from here:*

A. *Follow Green Drive back to the A625, cross the road and retrace your steps to the car park.*

B. *Gain a higher level footpath above Burbage Edge and follow this along the top of the crags - with a 1/4 mile break about half way along- back to the A625.*

C. *Follow Green Drive to a point a little way past the southern edge of the plantation below, then turn right along a footpath leading to an old stone packhorse bridge at the corner of the plantation. Turn left and walk alongside the stream, then regain Green Drive and retrace your steps to the car park.*

The rock that provides the sport is a coarse sandstone. Around 250 million years ago, this area was part of a massive river delta. Over a period of time, the sand deposited by the river was compressed by the weight of further deposits. This, in turn, generated the heat that transformed the sand into solid rock. Earth movement later tilted these sedimentary bands of rock to expose the abrupt 'edges' which have since been weathered by the forces of nature. This type of sandstone was used in past centuries for grinding and sharpening cutlery and farm tools. Partly worked and abandoned millstones can be seen in the quarries near the end of the walk.

Refreshments   Mobile supplies of various kinds at Upper Burbage Bridge.
Fox House Inn. Beer garden, pub food available.
National Trust cafe at Longshaw, near Fox House Inn

D. *As for C to the footpath going down to the packhorse bridge but, instead, bear left off Green Drive and pick your way amongst large boulders to reach the old quarries. Continue along the quarry track to gain the A625 a little above Green Drive.*

SHORTER VARIATION
i. *As for 1 to 3 above as far as the northwest exit from Carl Wark, then: Turn right immediately beyond the exit and follow a footpath which skirts around the crags that form the northern boundary of the fort. Continue down to the old stone packhorse bridge mentioned in C above, then up to Green Drive. Cross the track and continue as for D above.*

ACCESS BY BUS
To Fox House from Sheffield (S. Y. T. & Trent)

BLACKCAP
grey and white with a black cap - 14cm

Dearne Valley and Barnburgh

Outline Dearne Bridge ~ High Melton ~ Barnburgh Cliff ~ Barnburgh ~ Harlington ~ Dearne Bridge

Summary A fine excursion in some of the more attractive countryside between Doncaster and Dearne. Starting at Denaby Ings Nature Reserve, a steady climb leads up to the estate village of High Melton From here, the ascent continues through farmland to the top of an escarpment and, along this section, the views are extensive After descending to Barnburgh, a village with ancient origins, a pleasant stroll down to and along the banks of the River Dearne leads easily back to the Nature Reserve. Apart from a very short section near High Melton, well-defined footpaths and tracks are used throughout.

Attractions At Denaby Ings Nature Reserve there is a small visitor centre, where information on the birds that visit the 'ings', or water- meadows, can be obtained. Nearby is a hide, where a pair of binoculars would be an asset Even without them, however, you might pick out pochard, tufted duck, mallard and grebe.

If you can tear yourselves away from this delightful spot, a trek along field footpaths leads up to the estate village of High Melton, which has been a settlement at least since Roman times The village is left by a farm track that crosses an enormous field of crops. This area, flanked by the conurbations of Barnsley to the west and Doncaster to the east, is part of a rich agricultural region that has escaped industrial colonisation This particular field is at the top of an escarpment, and the views are extensive on a clear day In the spring, when the crops are no more than seedlings, partridge are more easily sighted than at other times of the year, although their pale brown colouring is still a very effective camouflage.

After the prairie-like fields, the strip of woodland alongside Barnburgh Cliff provides a welcome contrast Such stretches of woodland in areas where most of the land has come under the plough are a haven for many species of birds and other wildlife, and it is worth spending a little time identifying some of these and examining the variety of food sources in this small area. The 'cliff' is an outcrop of Magnesium Limestone along the top of an escarpment that stretches from Conisbrough northwards through High Melton, Hickleton and Hooton Pagnell

Leaving Barnburgh Cliff, a descent is made to the village of Barnburgh, with its interesting old stone farm buildings and cottages.

continued on page 64

61

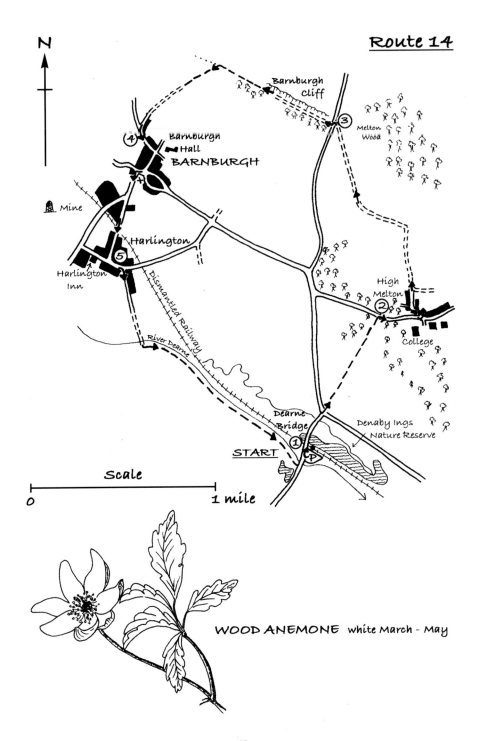

N

Barnburgh Cliff

④ Barnburgh Hall
BARNBURGH

③ Melton Wood

Mine

Harlington

⑤

Harlington Inn

Dismantled Railway

High Melton
② College

River Dearne

Dearne Bridge

Denaby Ings Nature Reserve

START ①
P

Scale

0   1 mile

WOOD ANEMONE   white March - May

Route 14
Dearne Valley and Barnburgh

5½miles

START   *At Dearne Bridge, 1 mile east of Mexborough on the minor road that links Mexborough with Sprotbrough. Park at the official Nature Reserve car park on the north side of the River Dearne. (G. R. 498008)*

ROUTE

1. *On leaving the car park walk north to where Cadeby Road joins on the right. On the corner facing is a Public Footpath sign. Follow in the direction of the sign along an ascending field footpath. After crossing a footbridge, go left a little then continue uphill in the same direction as before. After crossing two stiles you join a road. (The right of way may have been ploughed on parts of this section but the direction is fairly obvious.)*

2. *Turn right at the road and walk along the pavement into High Melton. Turn left along Hangman Stone Lane, which is opposite the entrance to the college. Continue along the lane, forking right at Box Tree House. After the houses, a track is joined. Continue along the track in the same direction. Follow it for a mile to a minor road.*

3. *Turn left, then right immediately at a Public Bridleway sign. Follow the bridleway below Barnburgh Cliff. After ¾mile the bridleway forks left downhill. Follow this to a road on the outskirts of Barnburgh.*

4. *Turn left and walk along High Street to the centre of the village. Continue on the right of the church down Church Lane. Stay on Church Lane when the main road bends right. Go down to a T-junction. (Harlington Inn is 200 metres to the right.)*

5. *Turn left along Doncaster Road and, in a short distance, right down Mill Lane. Follow the lane to a footbridge over the River Dearne. Cross it, then go left along the riverside footpath. On reaching the Mexborough Sprotbrough road turn left to finish. (After crossing the Dearne, the first half mile alongside the river is not a right of way. Should this be barred to the public for some reason, after crossing the footbridge carry straight on to the second stepping stile - the first one being redundant - then turn left along a narrow footpath that keeps right of a dike. This leads back to the riverside.)*

Also, on the outskirts of the village is small walled enclosure, Barnburgh Pinfold. An inscription reads: " an enclosure where stray animals were impounded until claimed has existed on this site since Medieval times". Barnburgh was originally an Anglo-Saxon settlement. The church is Norman, dating from the 12th century. On the church tower a cat is carved. According to tradition, Sir Percival Cresacre, the local landlord, died in 1477 after being attacked by a wildcat in the church porch!

The way back from Barnburgh is alongside a man-made diversion of the River Dearne. The word 'dearne' derives from the Celtic for deer. There are no deer hereabouts these days but various species of waterside birds can be seen.

Refreshments   Harlington Inn at Harlington. Beer garden

Stone Cross at Cawthorne

Route 15

Roche Abbey and Laughton-en-le-Morthen

Outline   Roche Abbey ~ King's Wood ~ Laughton-en-le-Morthen ~
Slade Hooton ~ Roche Abbey

Summary   A pleasant walk in a quiet rural enclave of industrial South
Yorkshire. Starting in a secluded little valley by the ruins of Roche Abbey,
a footpath leads up through woods and out into farmland en route to
Laughton-en-le-Morthen, a village whose history goes back to the Vikings.
From Laughton, there are exceptionally good views west towards the
Pennines. The way back is mostly downhill along field footpaths to regain
the woods and the grounds of the abbey.

Attractions Although only a mile from the mining town of Maltby, the
setting of Roche Abbey in a wooded valley flanked by limestone cliffs is
more reminiscent of the White Peak of Derbyshire. The abbey was founded
in 1147 for the Cistercian Order by Richard de Busli and Richard Fitsturgis-
- the two men owned land on opposite sides of the stream that runs through
the valley. It is one of the earliest examples of Gothic architecture in England.
After the dissolution of the abbey in 1539, the buildings were pillaged, and
later 'quarrying' of the stone for nearby cottages and farmhouses has left
the barest skeleton of the fine building that once stood here. What remains,
however, is well worth exploring, and children can do this here without the
usual constraints imposed upon them in their investigation of Our past
heritage.

   Just behind the ruin, where the walk starts proper, is a delightful little
waterfall with stepping stones and a pond above it. These features, and
the grounds as a whole, were landscaped in the 18th century by Capability
Brown, better known for his accomplishments at Chatsworth. And as at
Chatsworth, the flora is more diverse than it would have been had it been
left to nature alone. Of particular note are the numerous yews, wellingtonias
and green hellebore.

   On emerging from the wooded valley into the rich arable farmland
above, the vista opens out and the views are extensive. On a clear day, the
Pennine hills to the west can be picked out, whilst to the east distant power
stations dominate the skyline.

   In the nearer distance, attesting to its past significance, is the magnificent
medieval church spire at Laughton-en-le-Morthen, which rises to 185
feet. The original church on the site was Anglo-Saxon but was rebuilt by
the Normans in the 12th century and refashioned in the 14th century. Just

continued on page 68

65

Route 15

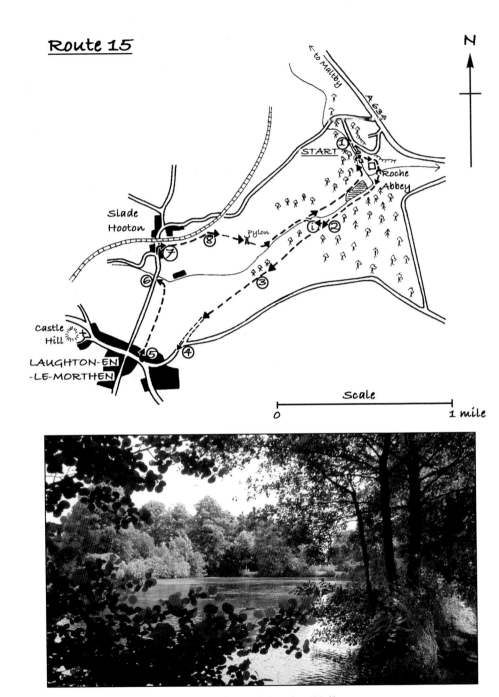

Old Mill Pond, Loxley Valley

Route 15

Roche Abbey and Laughton-en-le-Morthen   4½ miles

(Shorter Variation 1½miles)

START   *At Roche Abbey car park, signposted off the A634 2 miles southeast of Maltby. (G.R. 542901)*

ROUTE

1. *From the car park adjacent to the stream, walk towards Roche Abbey, passing through an ancient arched gateway, to pick up the footpath that follows the left-hand perimeter fence of the abbey. Follow this all the way around, then cross a stream and continue up to a man-made waterfall. Stay on the left of the waterfall and the pond above it, following the woodland footpath to a fork in about 1/2 mile.*

2. *Take the left fork uphill to two wooden stiles which are redundant since the removal of a fence. Enter the field ahead and walk along its right-hand boundary with a hedge on the right. Continue to the remains of a metal kissing gate.*

3. *Bear right past the gate and continue along the edge of another field in the same general direction. The footpath eventually joins a track. Continue straight on along this to where it meets a narrow country lane.*

4. *Turn right and follow the lane (Firbeck Lane) to a junction with the main road through Laughton (St. John's Road). Turn right here and walk as far as the St. Leger Arms on the right. (Keep straight on for the church, etc. then retrace your steps).*

5. *Turn right into the pub car park and go through the beer garden to pick up a signposted footpath on the far side. Continue along this, keeping close to the hedge on the right, as far as a stream. Turn left and pass beneath a pipe to gain a minor road.*

6. *Turn right at the road and walk uphill into Slade Hooton as far as the railway bridge.*

7. *Turn right at the signposted footpath by the bridge and follow the footpath alongside the railway line for just over 1/4 mile to another Public Footpath sign.*

8. *Bear right across an enormous field, heading for an electricity pylon in the distance (the right of way may be ploughed). After the pylon, continue in the same direction to a stream, then go left alongside the stream. In about 1/2 mile, a footbridge on the right is reached. The right of way crosses the footbridge to pick up the footpath used on the outward journey at the fork mentioned in 2 above. From here, you can retrace your steps back to the car park.*

beyond the western edge of the churchyard is the overgrown earthwork of a motte and bailey castle. Laughton was most likely a Viking administrative centre, since 'Morthen' is Old Scandinavian for 'the moorland district with a common assembly'.

Opposite the north side of the church is another interesting building, the village school. It was built at some time between 1610 and 1619 and is reckoned to be the oldest surviving school building in the county.

A short distance from Laughton, the walk passes through Slade Hooton. Again, the name tells a lot about the origins of the settlement. In Anglo-Saxon, 'Hoo' meant a spur of land and 'ton' a farmstead. Thus, the original settlement was a farmstead on a spur of land. There are several places in this part of South Yorkshire with Hooton in the name.

From Slade Hooton, a pleasant ramble through cornfields woods leads back to the grounds of the abbey.

Refreshments   St. Leger Arms at Laughton. Beer garden.
Hatfield Arms at Laughton.

Alternatively, continue straight on along a concessionary footpath which stays on the left of the stream and the pond. Continue to and across a bridge adjacent to Abbey House and so back to the start.

SHORTER VARIATION
i.   *As for 1 above. then fork right and continue to and across a footbridge. Turn right here and continue as for the alternative in 8 above. (1½ miles)*

Lesser Celandine yellow, March-May

68

4½ miles
(Shorter variation 3½ miles)

Chesterfield Canal -- Shireoaks to Thorpe Salvin

Outline   Shire oaks ~ Turner wood ~ Thorpe Salvin ~ Nether Thorpe ~ Shireoaks

Summary   A first rate walk with lots of interest and best done in spring because of the abundance of wildflowers to be seen en route. From Shireoaks, a towpath is followed along what is probably the most picturesque section of the disused Chesterfield canal. On leaving the canal, a footpath leads through woodland into the ancient village of Thorpe Salvin. The way back is along a mixture of quiet country lanes and footpaths across farmland, and an airfield for light aircraft is passed on the way.

Attractions   Although Shireoaks, where the walk starts and finishes, is in Nottinghamshire, the excursion is mostly within South Yorkshire. Besides, this is one of the prettiest walks in this guide, and it would have been a pity to omit it just because its 'natural' starting point was in the wrong county!

On leaving Nottinghamshire, the canal and its towpath are soon reached. Here begins a succession of narrow locks behind each of which the canal has silted up and formed reed-lined shallow ponds of slow- moving water that ducks find to their taste. Alongside the towpath, a mixture of hazel, sycamore and bramble form the edge of woodland. With a bit of luck, blackcap may be sighted along this section.   The towpath passes through Turnerwood, a tiny hamlet in a most picturesque setting. On a plaque on the bridge here, the history of the canal is described in some detail. Work on the canal was begun in 1771 by James Brindley. After its completion in 1777, it provided a waterway link from Chesterfield to the Humber estuary , along which lead, coal and iron were transported for shipping out. The link west of Worksop became disused in 1908 after the collapse of the Norwood Tunnel, 3 miles upstream from Turnerwood.

On leaving the towpath, a footpath is followed through Old Spring Wood, where wild flowers grow in abundance. Amongst the beech, hawthorn and sycamore you should find wood anemone, wood sorrel, violet, celandine and primrose and many more species.

From this lovely spot, a short walk leads up into Thorpe Salvin, a very attractive village with some interesting old buildings. 'Thorpe' is Old Danish for an outlying settlement, whilst 'Salvin' was the name of the manorial Norman lords who resided here. The church is Norman and houses a remarkable font from that period. The ruined hall was built by Henry

continued on page 72

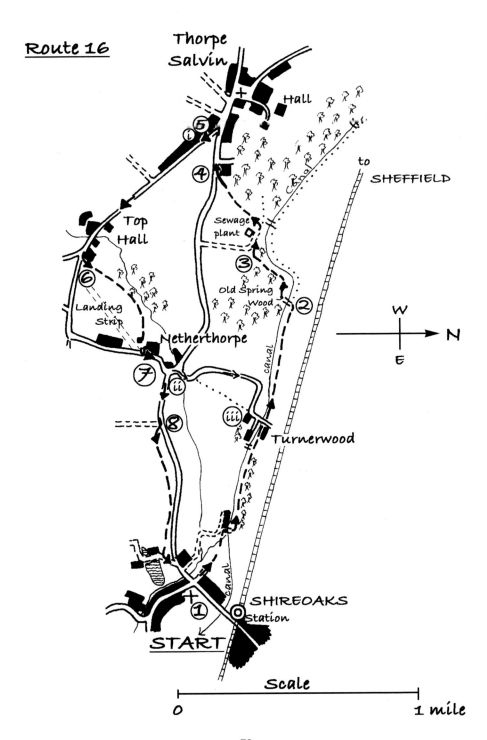

Route 16

Thorpe Salvin

Hall

to SHEFFIELD

Top Hall

Sewage plant

Old Spring Wood

canal

Landing Strip

Netherthorpe

W
N
E

Turnerwood

SHIREOAKS
Station

canal

START

Scale

0   1 mile

70

Route 16
Chesterfield Canal -- Shireoaks to Thorpe Salvin   4½ miles
(Shorter variation 3½ miles)

START   *Park near St. Luke's Church in Shireoaks. (G.R.553809)*

ROUTE

1. *Almost immediately opposite the church, at the south end of Shireoaks Row, take the Public Footpath signposted to Turnerwood. Go past a pond and continue to a bridge over the canal. Cross the bridge, turn left and follow the towpath to the hamlet of Summerwood. Pass under the brick bridge and carry on along the towpath to another brick bridge dated 1835.*

2. *Cross this bridge and follow the footpath into woods, branching right where there are other possibilities. On emerging from the wood, a bend in a track is reached.*

3. *Turn right here and continue to the sewage plant on the left. Follow the perimeter fence of the plant as it bends left uphill with a hedge bordering the footpath on the right. Continue to a minor road at Thorpe Salvin.*

4. *Turn right at the road and walk to the junction with Common Road. (The arish Oven is a little further on the right.)*

5. *Turn left and continue along Common Road. About 1/2 mile after leaving the village the lane dips into the tiny hamlet of Top Hall. Continue up the other side of the dip as far as the last building on the left, just beyond which is a Public Footpath sign on the left.*

6. *Turn left here and walk diagonally across the field ahead, aiming for the right edge of a wood on the far side of the field. The footpath bears right before an open gateway near a pill box, then continues alongside the airfield at Netherthorpe. Keeping a hedge on the left, continue to a country lane in Netherthorpe.*

7. *Turn left and walk down the lane to a T-junction. Turn right and follow the minor road for about 1/3 mile to a farm track and stile on the right.*

8. *Cross the stile and continue alongside the wall on the left, thus keeping parallel with the road. Although there is access to the road at several points, it is safer to continue along the right of way as far as a track leading to a large house with a large pond at its frontage. (The track is a right of way, enabling closer investigation of the pond's wildlife.) Turn left, then right at the road to finish.*

Sandford in the 16th century and abandoned at the end of the 17th century when the owners built a new house at Kiveton Park. Holding more sway with the youngsters, the village pub has a large beer garden with an assortment of playground apparatus.

On the way back, the walk picks up a field footpath that skirts the edge of an airfield belonging to Sheffield Aero Club. Watching the light aircraft take off and land - and this at very close quarters --will provide amusement. And whilst you are getting bored waiting for the next piece of action, cast your eye on the hedgerows where you may spot yellowhammer and wren. There is further interest for the keen birdwatcher not far from the end of the walk, where large ponds have been colonised by geese and other waterside birds.

Refreshments Parish Oven public house at Thorpe Salvin. Family room

---

SHORTER VARIATION

Start at Thorpe Salvin. Park on Common Road.

i.   *As for 5, 6 and 7 above as far as the T -junction at Netherthorpe.*

ii. *Turn left at the T -junction, then first right along a cul-de-sac signposted to Turnerwood. Either follow the lane to Turnerwood or, at the first left-hand bend, go straight on along a field footpath to the hamlet.*

iii. *At Turnerwood, turn left after crossing the bridge and follow the canal towpath to the bridge dated 1835. Continue as for 2, 3 and 4 above.*

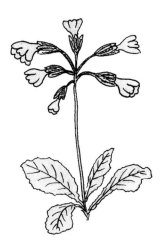

Cowslip April - May (Yellow)

Appendices

ROUTES IN ORDER OF DIFFICULTY

The walks are arranged into three categories according to distance, and within each category they are listed in order of difficulty. Difficulty is assessed on the basis of how strenuous the walks are relative to others in the same category .

Shorter Walks (up to 3½ miles)

Route   4:   —   *Worsbrough Mill Country Park (Variation III)* — *1¼ miles*
Route 11:   —   *Loxley Valley (Variation II)* — *1¼ miles*
Route 15:   —   *Roche Abbey & Laughton-en-le-Morthen (Variation)* — *1½ miles*
Route   4:   —   *Worsbrough Mill Country Park (Variation II)* — *2¼ miles*
Route 16:   —   *Chesterfield Canal (Variation)* — *3½ miles*
Route   4:   —   *Worsbrough Mill Country Park (Variation I)* — *2½ miles*
Route   5:   —   *Langsett Reservoir& Midhope Moor (Variation)* — *3½ miles*
Route   6:   —   *Green Moor & Upper Don V alley (Variation I)* — *2¼ miles*
Route 12:   —   *Rivelin Valley (Variation)* — *2½ miles*
Route 13:   —   *Burbage Valley (Variation)* — *2½ miles*
Route 11:   —   *Loxley Valley (Variation I)* — *2¾ miles*
Route   6:   —   *Green Moor & Upper Don Valley (Variation II)* — *3 miles*

Medium Length Walks (more than 3½ and less than 5 miles)

Route 16:   —   *Chesterfield Canal* — *4½ miles*
Route 15:   —   *Roche Abbey & Laughton-en-le-Morthen* — *4½ miles*
Route   8:   —   *Bolsterstone & Whitwell Moor (Variation)* — *4 miles*
Route   4:   —   *Worsbrough Mill Country Park* — *4½ miles*
Route   1:   —   *Cannon Hall, Deffer Wood & Cawthorne* — *4¾ miles*
Route 11:   —   *Loxley Valley* — *4½ miles*
Route 10:   —   *Bradfield Dale & Dale Dike Reservoir* — *4½ miles*
Route 13:   —   *Burbage Valley* — *4½ miles*
Route 12:   —   *Rivelin Valley* — *4 miles*
Route   6:   —   *Green Moor & Upper Don Valley* — *4¼ miles*
Route   9:   —   *Spout House Hill & Hollin Edge Height (Variation II)* — *4 miles*
Route   9:   —   *Spout House Hill & Hollin Edge Height (Variation I)* — *4¾ miles*

Longer Walks (5 or more miles)

Route 14:   —   *Dearne Valley & Barnburgh* — *5½ miles*
Route   2:   —   *Kine Moor & Silkstone Fall* — *5 miles*
Route   7:   —   *Mill Moor, Hermit Hill & Wortley Park* — *5½ miles*
Route   5:   —   *Langsett Reservoir & Midhope Moor* — *5 miles*
Route   8:   —   *Bolsterstone & Whitwell Moor* — *5 miles*
Route   3:   —   *Royd Moor &Hartcliff Hill* — *6 miles*
Route   9:   —   *Spout House Hill & Hollin Edge Height* — *6 miles*

COUNTRY PARKS

Cannon Hall Country Park 5 miles west of Barnsley on the A635 and 1 mile northwest of Cawthorne. Large area of parkland with woods, lakes and grassland. Interesting collection of water-birds. Gardens surround Cannon Hall Museum.

Cusworth Country Park 2 miles northwest of Doncaster off the Al. Woodland, gardens and parkland surround Cusworth Hall Museum. Grounds have a natural history trail and ornamental lake.

Farm Park in Graves Park, Sheffield. Large collection of rare and ornamental waterfowl. 25 acres of pasture and paddock contain a whole range of cattle, sheep and pigs, some very rare.

Howell Wood Country Park 7 miles northeast of Barnsley and 1 mile southeast of South Kirby. Woodland walks.

Rother Valley Country Park at Wales Bar, 8 miles southeast of Sheffield. Entrance is off A618 between Killamarsh and Wales Bar. Landscaped recreation park. Network of footpaths and cycle routes with picnic sites. Leisure facilities include sailing, canoeing, windsurfing, rowing, water-skiing, horse riding, model-boating. Wetlands with interesting wildfowl.

Thrybergh Country Park 1 mile north of Thrybergh off A630. Landscaped recreation park. Water sports and fishing. Nature Reserve, refuge for wildfowl.

Wentworth Park 3 miles northeast of Chapeltown on B6090. Deer park and lakes with interesting wildfowl.

Worsbrough Mill Country Park 2½ miles south of Barnsley town centre. Includes a reservoir, mixed deciduous woodland, wetland and open grassland. Bird reserve, relics of metal working industry and coal-mining, and a working water-powered corn mill. Open all year round.

NATURE RESERVES

Broomhill Flash 5 miles southeast of Barnsley off the B6273. 10 acres of standing water surrounded by farmland. Interesting birdlife.

Denaby Ings Northeast of Mexborough off A6023. See Route 14. Large areas of standing water with marshland. Noted for birdlife and insect life. Hide by waterside.

Potteric Carr 2½ miles southeast of Doncaster. Nature Reserve. Extensive areas of water, marsh, woodland and reed fen. Wide variety of trees, wildflowers, butterflies and moths. Over 130 species of bird seen each year. Restricted access. Contact Yorkshire Naturalist Trust Ltd., 20 Castlegate, York, YO1 1RP.

Rother Valley Country Park Wetlands with interesting wildfowl.

Sandall Beat Wood to the east of Doncaster, approx. 2 miles from town Unrestricted access. Woodland and fen with large variety of wildflowers, ferns, moths and butterflies. Over 100 species of bird sighted.

Thrybergh Country Park 1 mile north of Thrybergh off A630. Nature Reserve, refuge for wildfowl.

Worsborough Mill Country Park 2½ miles south of Barnsley. Bird reserve.

NATURE TRAILS/NATURAL HISTORY WALKS

Sheffield City Council/Countryside Commission have produced detailed leaflets with suggested walks and natural history notes on the Loxley and Shirebrook Valleys. are available from Sheffield Central Library .

Rivelin Valley Nature Trail. A 2 mile long trail starting at Rivelin Post Office and following the River Rivelin eastwards towards Malin Bridge. Includes dams, weirs and ruined workshops, and the riverside is rich in birdlife with a large variety of wildflowers.

MUSEUMS AND PLACES OF HISTORICAL INTEREST

Abbeydale Industrial Hamlet Off Abbeydale Road, Beauchief, Sheffield. Restored steel and scythe works dating from the late 18th century. Water-powered. Working days as advertised. Cafe.

Bishop's House Museum On south side of Sheffield in Meersbrook Park. Fine example of a timber-framed house built around 1500. Two rooms furnished in the style of a prosperous yeoman's home of 17th century.

Cannon Hall Museum 6 miles west of Barnsley off A635. (See Route 1) Set in Cannon Hall Country Park. 18th century house with displays of furniture, paintings, glassware, silver, pewter and pottery . Military section traces history of 13th/18th Royal Hussars. Conisbrough Castle The keep is one of the finest examples of 12th century building in England.

Cusworth Hall Museum On the outskirts of Doncaster, 1/2 mile west of A638 2 miles north of town centre. Contains many interesting relics of Yorkshire life.

Doncaster Museum & Art Gallery Contains many relics of Roman times in Doncaster as well as geological and natural history items and costume.

Fire Museum West Bar, Sheffield. Opened in 1900 as a police/fire station. Display of fire appliances dating from 1794 to 1942. Cobbled yard, garage and stables, police station and cells, breathing apparatus room, display room. Museum shop, cafe and children's area.

Kelham Island (Sheffield Industrial Museum) Tells story of Sheffield's industrial evolution. Houses huge 12000 h.p. River Don steam engine and 150 h. p. Crossley Gas engine, both of which can be seen in operation. 'Little Mester's Workshops' where traditional self -employed craftsmen in the cutlery trade carry on their normal business. Film shows. Cafe. Situated by River Don off Alma Street.

Monk Bretton Priory Ruins of medieval monastery. 2 miles northeast of Barnsley. The ruins are extensive and include a largely intact gatehouse built in the early 15th century.

Sheffield City Museum & Mappin Art Gallery In Weston Park. Large museum with good stock of exhibits. Fine natural history, geology and archaeology displays. Cafe.

Shepherd Wheel in Whiteley Woods. Overshot waterwheel run regularly. Formerly cutler's grinding mill.

Roche Abbey 2 miles south of Maltby off A634. Impressive ruins of medieval monastery. Very attractive setting (see Route 15).

Rockley Engine House West of Birdwell and on Birdwell to Dodworth road. (See Route 4) Built in 1813 to drain local iron workings. Free to investigate.

Rockley Blast Furnace Ruins are near Engine House hidden amongst trees. Constructed in 1652, and fuelled by charcoal, It is thought the furnace may be the oldest surviving example in Europe .

Worsbrough Mill Museum Built in about 1625, originally a water-powered corn mill. Now a restored working mill producing its own flour. Bird reserve and hide on west coast of reservoir.

Wortley Top Forge 1 mile south of Thurgoland and west of Wortley off A629. (See Route 7).17th century ironworks situated in the picturesque Upper Don Valley. Only example of an 18th century water-powered hammer set in a forge. On several occasions during the year it stages a display of working engines, local crafts, and other attractions. Large collection of steam engines, miniature railway and refreshments.

Wyming Brook

On the March, Cannon Hall Country Park

Heron

Water Pump at Bolsterstone